ESCAPE FROM THE BEDSIDE

SHARON BALTMAN MD

Escape From The Bedside

Copyright © 2013 Sharon Baltman

Spelling throughout follows British/Canadian usage.

CONTENTS

PART 2   FACE À FACE WITH LIFE

For my dear mother Hellie,
who tirelessly taught me
"to stand on my own two feet."

Introduction

One recent summer evening I joined a group of old friends at a local watering hole to hear one of our buddies sing and strum the guitar. We were getting re-acquainted, laughing at old jokes as I downed my second rum and coke, when suddenly the owner/waitress slipped and fell. All eyes turned to me. I remained frozen in my seat. "To be or not to be… a doctor?" the old ambivalent thought raced through my head.

Such scenarios continued to play out in my life as I learned to deal with the ramifications of my 1964 decision to apply to medical school. First, the hard work and competition in university, then the outrage of older male colleagues taking advantage of me, later witnessing their dismissal of patients' voices. Forced to find a way to navigate the system to find peace for myself, understanding for patients, and freedom to practise in an equitable way, I ultimately learned to tailor my professional practice to suit my values and principles, rather than allow the profession to rule me.

I found emergency work unsatisfying, as I barely met the patients and rarely saw them a second time. I moved into general practice to have longer-term connections, but ran out of time trying to deal with both physical and emotional needs. In order to hear more about peoples' lives and what made them tick, I finally chose full-time psychotherapy work so I could have time to listen to their tales in a quiet, unrushed venue. I also needed time to devote to raising my daughter, later becoming a single mom. While I started with classic Freudian analytic work, I later moved into cognitive behavioural therapy, to teach patients to deal with the here-and-now in a concrete way, to re-frame their thoughts more positively, and to find the grey zone between the black and white extremes of life.

More recently, I was attracted by Narrative Medicine, the field of work based on the importance of listening to the patient's story—wherein the doctor does not ask the question: 'Where is your pain?' but rather inquires: 'What do I need to know about you?' The first definitive textbook on the subject was published in 2006 by an internist, Dr Rita Charon of Columbia University. I used one of its techniques called Therapeutic Writing, which involves encouraging people to 'just write a story'. By creating a narrative that others can relate to, patients begin to make sense of the pieces of their lives so they can move forward with understanding and coherence in response to themselves and others.

This memoir is written for anyone, patient or doctor, who loves stories. It tracks adventures that were grist for my mill at home and at the office, from which I tried to create a life that was healthy both personally and professionally. After many years of listening to the narratives of others, it was time to write a story to make sense of my own life.

Author's Note

In order to protect confidentiality, exact locations, names and defining characteristics of patients and doctors have been changed. Details in the stories consist of composites in order to make patients and doctors unrecognizable. However, all encounters were real.

PART I
FACE À FACE WITH DOCTORS

CHAPTER 1

The Winding Road

My first exposure to a doctor was our family physician who had delivered me. Max Finestine, old, short and bald, with a round wrinkled face and thick brown glasses, always wore an oversized scruffy suit with a bow-tie, spoke English with a thick German accent and carted around a heavy, worn leather bag that never closed. I was five years old and in bed with a high fever and the chicken pox when I heard the dreaded voice coming from downstairs, followed by sounds of him clomping up the steps, huffing and puffing. I wanted to hide, but was too sick to move.

He burst into my tiny room, filling it with his smell of rubbing alcohol mixed with cigarette smoke.

"Hello young lady, you are not so vell, I see."

He pinched my cheek between his second and third knuckles as he always did. I hated it. I glared at him. He poked and prodded my belly and chest with his cold hands, touching my spots, which made them itch even more. He picked at one scab and threw it across the floor. The spot began to bleed.

"She's a pretty sick little girl," he said quietly to my mother. "I have to give her some penicillin. I think she has an infection on top of her chicken pox."

He rummaged around in his black bag and I knew what was coming when I saw the needle.

"Not again!" I yelped, using my last bit of energy to jump out of bed and hide behind my red upholstered doll's couch in the corner of my room. He came after me. I took off, screaming all the way down the stairs and into the living room where I collapsed behind the drapes. But he found me again and grabbing me by the waist, jabbed me with the needle. It stung my bum. I was sobbing and shaking, but he hardly seemed to notice, hardly seemed to care.

He stuffed his things back into his bag, turned to my mother and said, "Sorry, Mrs Baltman, but I had to get the penicillin into her. She'll be fine in a few days." Dr Finestine stood there, as if waiting to be offered a cup of tea.

Instead, my mother went into the kitchen, cut him a piece of her delicious chocolate cake with icing that I was too sick to eat and wrapping it up, she thanked him for coming and ushered him out.

After closing the door, she bent down, took me in her arms and said, "He gets a bit gruff when people don't listen to him. You'll soon be feeling better and the next time you see him, you won't need a needle. Come on, let's go back up to bed. I'll make you some cream of wheat with the yellow floating blobs that you like and some sweet tea." I took her hand reluctantly and we headed upstairs together.

The one advantage of the horrible experience with Dr Finestine was that I got a rare moment alone with my mother. I usually had to share her with my older brother and sister and my father who was not at home a lot.

He worked late, so we rarely saw him for dinner and sometimes didn't see him before we went to bed. But on Saturdays my father took the three of us out in the car, down to what he called *the shop*, a factory on Dundas Street East where we got to bounce on bales of felt. His company manufactured fillings for mattresses. We weren't allowed to go near the spring-making machines because some of my father's workers had lost fingers in them, but we did get to ride up and down in the huge freight elevator with the rattling criss-cross gate. Only my brother or an older cousin could operate that. We had the run of the place when the workers weren't there and even snooped around the treasures in my father's office. He didn't smoke, but his brother and business partner, my Uncle Jack, did. Next to the desk, standing on the floor, was a silver ashtray lined in black glass. On it was written: "Ashes to ashes, dust to dust, I am here to collect ashes and butts."

After *the shop* we would stop for cherry pie at the Sip and Bite restaurant on Parliament Street, then drive to my grandmother's house on Crawford, north of College, to join Uncle Jack and his sister, Auntie Bella, in front of the television, a black and white one in a wooden console. This TV provided the only English spoken in the room. My father, aunt, uncle and *Bubby* (grandmother) talked Yiddish together: "*Soogt er... soogt er.*" (He said... he said). Although my father's side of the family came from Poland, they rarely spoke Polish. Yiddish was all I ever heard from them.

My Auntie Bella had been the first to come to Canada from Poland with her husband in the 1920s. She offered to sponsor the rest of her siblings, but only succeeded in bringing three brothers. The two others refused, as they were already 'established' in Poland. And they, their wives and children, perished in Treblinka. But no one ever spoke about them. We were just an ordinary, happy, North American family prospering in Canada in the early 1950s.

In the car on the way home from *Bubby's* house, my father taught us a song about walking into the forest and hearing the birds singing—a mélange of Hebrew, Yiddish and Polish:

Ivaya hoolachti, kol tziporah shumati, echad gezingen li- li- li,
Tsveita hot gesingen choh-choh-choh.
Posodchloh dolyasa, yeden shpeeva, nugleesa,
Yeden shpeeva nugleesymbol,
Yeden shpeeva si-si-si.

My early love of language propelled me towards wanting a career as a linguist. I learned Hebrew in a primary day school, studied French from grade 8, Latin from grade 9, and German from grade 10, and dreamed of becoming a translator at the United Nations in New York City. When I went to see a high school guidance counsellor for help with my future plans, my stern language teacher, Miss Drummond, dashed all hope of such an ambitious career. She assured me the best I could hope for was teaching. In those days girls either became teachers, nurses, or secretaries, or got married and had kids. I didn't want any of that.

Having no desire to turn out like my spinster teacher of languages, I quickly switched to maths and sciences, which I aced. To this day, I can't remember why I chose medicine, except that it seemed to be the only path that *didn't* lead to teaching.

I decided to apply for Pre-Medicine at the University of Toronto, for September 1965.

My mother was fully behind me. "You need a career so you can always be independent and stand on your own two feet. Not like me. I've had to depend entirely upon your father."

When my father's family got wind of my plans, Auntie Bella's response was: "If she becomes a doctor, she'll only be able to marry another doctor, so that means she'll never get married."

Whatever her rationale, my father picked up on his elder sister's negative point of view and he tried to discourage me, too. "You'll be in school for a long time. What do you need it for? You could get your BA and be a teacher like your sister. What's so terrible about that? Your cousin Annie only got a BA. It was good enough for her."

"But will you pay for me to go to medical school? That's what I need to know. I can't afford to go if I have to pay for it all myself. I can work all summer, but I won't have time for my studies if I have to work during the school year as well. If I go to school in Toronto I can live at home and save money that way..." I attempted to explain.

"*Ba meir kenst du walken.*" (As far as I'm concerned you can walk.) "I can't give you a car to get to school, but I can drive you down in the morning," he replied.

Confused, I tried again. "Harry, I'm not asking for a car or worrying about how to *get* to school. What I need to know is will you pay for my tuition and books, because otherwise I can't take the spot if I get accepted into pre-med."

"We'll see," was all he said.

I started calling my parents by their first names when I was sixteen. It was just something I did and Harry and Helen both received it with good humour and love.

I knew Harry well and I learned to play his game—push him a bit and lay off for a bit. We knew he loved us dearly and could only show it by bestowing or withholding money. If we chased him for money, he felt loved. By giving it, he was showing love. Coming from small town Poland, his range was limited. Any other kind of approval or acknowledgement, aside from joking banter, was alien to him. I danced his elaborate tango and he ultimately agreed to pay my tuition if accepted. He even offered to buy me a used car.

Memories of awful moments with Dr Finestine, whom I thought of as the scary absent-minded professor, returned to haunt me. Did I really want to be a part of that profession? Yet, the more opposition I heard, the more determined I became and the more opinions I sought.

I spoke to my older sister's boyfriend, George Molen, who was in his final year of medical school. "A girl like you with such big breasts doesn't belong in medical school," was all he said. I was outraged.

Hoping for some valuable input, I had a further discussion with a newly-graduated MD, Sidney, the older brother of my childhood friend Neil who lived across the street. He was nine years older than Neil and I, so we both looked up to him. He had given Neil his blessing for pre-med so I assumed he would support me, too.

"So, what do you think?" I casually inquired, hoping my nervousness didn't show.

"Do you want the truth?" he asked.

"I wouldn't be asking if I didn't want your answer."

"Look at your carefully manicured and painted fingernails."

"Ya, so what?" I asked, scanning my purple-tipped digits.

"You won't be able to keep those. You'll have to cut your nails short so you won't poke patients while examining them."

"So, what's your point?" I asked.

"Well, you enjoy things like that, *feminine* things. And, well... medicine just isn't a place for girls. It's hard work and... you have to stay up nights."

I stopped listening. I couldn't believe what I was hearing. I could have entertained any argument against medical school, but *not* the gender-based one.

My determination to become a doctor gelled—fast and hard. I had no more doubts: they had convinced me with their pathetic arguments against it that I must go to med school, if only to show them I could do it.

I had the grades, so all I had to do was pass my interview with the Dean and answer the one big question put to every female applicant to medical school at that time:

"Miss Baltman, how do you feel about the Three M's: Marriage, Motherhood and Medicine?"

"I feel fine," I recited my rehearsed answer. "Just like a male student, I will marry when I meet the right person. I will become a mother when I decide I want children. And I will practise medicine as my career."

"What about our loss if we invest valuable dollars in your education and then you quit to be a mother and stay at home? And you take a spot away from a man who would stay in medicine?"

"No one knows what will happen in the future. There are no guarantees that boys won't drop out. I hope to practise medicine for a very long time."

One month later, I received a letter of acceptance to the two-year Pre-Medicine course at the University of Toronto which then guaranteed entry into medical school for four more years.

Those two years of pre-med were filled with endless assignments, frequent exams and fiercely competitive classmates. I had serious doubts about continuing. Then the following year, our first of 'real' medical school, we were thick into our cadavers weeks before the arts kids started fall classes. And once they did start, they had time to sit out in the quadrangle lounging in the sun, while the med students beavered away in the dark basement of the anatomy building.

I was getting fed up with the long hours and the volume of work and finally made up my mind to quit. I even told my brother and sister-in-law about my decision. But then who turned up as my anatomy instructor but the same George Molen of the 'big breast' comment, now well-ensconced in my sister's past?

I told him I was ready to quit.

"You can't do that."

"Watch me. I've had it. I want to be out there socializing and having fun."

"Come on, let's go for a walk," he said, coaxing me out of the smelly lab into the fresh air.

"I'm serious, George, it's enough already. I've lost my scholarships over the past two years because I can't comprehend all the stats and biochemistry."

"You're past that now. Now is the real thing: bodies, living and dead; pharmacology, boring, but useful basics. You start to play doctor soon. Then you'll have a fabulous career."

"Come on, I can't believe you're saying this. You said the opposite to me before. And when you were in school, you were the biggest slacker," I retorted.

"You're right, I was. But I persisted and I'm glad I did. You won't regret it. And you could regret dropping out. Think about it."

"Ok. Ok. I'll think, but no promises. Can we go back into that stinky lab now before my buddies start looking for me?" I asked, heading for the heavy wooden doors.

"I'll see you down there later," George mumbled over his shoulder, running up the steps two at a time as I slowly descended the cold concrete stairs to my prison. I had some thinking to do.

Two weeks later, I called my brother: "Guess what? The weather turned cold so I stayed in school. I'm not quitting after all. George Molen talked me into staying."

"George Molen! I haven't heard that name for years," he replied. That was all he could muster, sounding just like our father.

"Yup," I replied, "I want to be a doctor."

CHAPTER 2

"California Here I Come..."

Towards the end of my sixth gruelling year of university, I was heading off to a two-month elective in warmer climes, with my boyfriend Jonathan, a classmate. I'd read about the Palo Alto Medical Clinic in California, a multi-specialty group practice, a novel concept at the time. They were taking on medical students to follow around general practitioners and paediatricians in their out-patient offices. On the home stretch of our final year, we would experience the first third of the medical aphorism: 'See one. Do one. Teach one.' It sounded perfect.

My family was supportive of my going to California for the elective, until I decided to drive. The old red Fiat 850 that my father had bought me to get back and forth from school was losing steam. Harry offered to take me shopping for a graduation present early, and I ended up with a second-hand pale blue Fiat hatchback.

"You can't possibly get across the U.S. in that thing," my older sister exclaimed. "And you and Jonathan aren't married, so you certainly can't live together once you get there!"

But I was determined, intent upon the opportunity of driving with Jonathan clear across the United States. The Fiat was the only way. We had Christmas holidays to get a head start on travel before our assignment began. Then a piston blew the day before we were due to leave Toronto. I was anxious to get going and being young and optimistic, we decided that we didn't mind a slow drive uphill, if we could 'let her rip' going down the other side.

Our modus operandi worked across many U.S. states, until another piston blew in Amarillo, Texas. The two remaining cylinders barely got us off the highway, let alone to our destination. Standing next to the car containing all our worldly possessions, we stuck out our thumbs to hitch a ride. A pick-up truck soon stopped and we hopped in, my jaw tightening at the sight of the rifle mounted above our seat. We got out at the nearest gas station, where we quickly arranged a tow.

Back at the station with our vehicle, amid the squeals of drills and smell of oil, awaiting the diagnosis and treatment recommendations, I questioned the wisdom of leaving home with only three cylinders. I had presumed we could get the car fixed electively in Palo Alto, not as an emergency in Amarillo, Texas.

Just then, the mechanic emerged, wiping his greasy hands on an even greasier chamois.

"It'll take three days to get 'er fixed," he said. "Them Fiat parts are tough to find right about here."

"Three days?" I asked in disbelief. I was devastated. What would we do for three days in Amarillo Texas? They offered us a ride to the closest motel and we signed ourselves in and settled into the seedy room to read, watch TV and eat on the cheap.

Jonathan and I had been dating for three years and at age 24, I thought of myself as a responsible adult. My mother trusted my decisions. My sister Rena did not. She was five years older than me and when I travelled with Jonathan to Europe the previous year, I couldn't tell her, or my father, although my mother knew. In the late '60s and '70s, living together without being married was still a taboo for many.

I'd known Jonathan since grade 10, but he had always been 'too suave' for me. We hadn't been in pre-med together, because he completed four years of undergraduate training in Biological and Medical Sciences, or 'B & M.' His group joined our class in second year medicine, knowing a lot more than we did, having spent two extra years 'cooking' all kinds of experiments. That's when Jonathan and I began to sit together in lectures, often with his neatly folded sports jacket resting across my lap. Most of the guys in my stream rarely wore a shirt and tie, let alone a jacket, but the B & M boys were more sophisticated, wearing both. In those days, universities were more formal and jeans were never worn. Dress code rebellion by the girls consisted of wearing white hospital uniform skirts very short, so they were the same length as our oversized white lab jackets.

How I had time to socialize with anyone in the midst of all that schoolwork, I don't know. But by February of second year medicine, while still dating other guys, I gave Jonathan a Valentine's Day card which read: *Do you want to be my Valentine?* and inside it said, *Take a number.* I thought it was very funny. He did not. That was my first clue that he had feelings for me. He was tall, dark, handsome, smart, and from B & M. At the time, I thought all I had going for me were big boobs and Jon had already told me that his older brother's advice was 'more than a handful is a waste'. I also knew that Jon hadn't liked me in high school because I was 'too smart'. His interest in me came as a surprise.

He made me laugh, we loved to dance and he kept me up-to-date on all the latest rock groups. Though buried under a tremendous workload, we dated exclusively. One side benefit was that if either of us missed a lecture, we could swap notes and procure each other copies of the hand-outs, instead of having to face one of our other classmates, who would inevitably resist, repeating the phrase, "Too much competition."

That refrain was the anthem of our class, a group of students who, from the age of 18, interacted six days a week between September 1st and June 30th for six years. From the very beginning, I had heard that there would be stiff competition, but I didn't pay much attention to it, until I met some of my 'rivals'. Most were male, as few women were accepted into medicine in those days. Classmates would do whatever they could to 'cut down on the competition' so that when marks were placed on a bell curve, 'if you could knock a few guys into the bottom of the heap, then your ass was safe' and you'd succeed from year to year.

Some would even compete to be the first one to leave an exam, which meant they knew their work cold, wrote it down fast and left early. After the first one walked out, the pressure on the rest of us in the room increased. The daily chatter between classes was about who got the better score, who did badly, who was a 'keener' or 'browner' and who was the last one to 'close' the library the night before. This pre-med stream has since been abolished and now everyone has to compete for acceptance into medical school from a four-year undergraduate science degree, so perhaps the students are more mature when they begin and are only together as a group for four years instead of six.

As the mechanic had predicted, after three days, the Fiat was ready to roll, just as the first snowstorm in years hit the Texas panhandle. White-outs across the highway threatened to stall us, but we forged ahead.

We ploughed through Albuquerque, New Mexico, on the way to overnight in Flagstaff, Arizona, driving through one town after another, each advertising its claim to fame: 'The Smelliest Town', 'The Town with the Largest Squash' or 'Home of the Giant Tomatoes'. Even with four cylinders restored, I found us stuck behind huge tractor-trailers on the long uphill stretches: our tiny Fiat sandwiched between two big Mack trucks.

Flagstaff may be dry, but it sure was cold, especially in January. Our battery gave out and we had to call the local motor league for a boost. They told us that the generator would re-charge it with all the driving we had to do throughout the day, so at least we didn't need a new one. We drove on into Nevada, 'The Driest State in the Nation', never stopping in the middle of the desert even when we hit Las Vegas. We finally made it to the California border, then as we drove westward to Castroville, 'The Artichoke Capital of the World', it got warmer, so our battery was no longer a problem.

At long last, we pulled into Palo Alto, cruised El Camino Real Boulevard from bottom to top, searching for accommodation close to the medical clinic. We finally found a 1970s-movie-style motel, with rooms on two levels opening onto an outdoor hallway, overlooking the swimming pool. We took a fully-furnished bachelor suite with kitchen facilities, including linens, telephone and housekeeping, which rented as 'cheap-by-the-week'. Parking the car down below, we dragged our stuff upstairs.

The next morning, I was shocked and disappointed to find that the overnight temperature in 'sunny California' had dipped below 30 degrees F. The Fiat wouldn't start again. By that point, we couldn't afford a new battery, so we just got another boost. We needed a functioning car to get us into the clinic in the centre of town and, of course, to take us up the coast to San Francisco.

My weekdays were filled with very civilized learning. Staff doctors treated me with great respect, contrary to my experience with more senior colleagues in hospitals at home. In Toronto medicine, you're always treated as a 'punk', meaning that no matter how many years you've put in, people in more senior positions always dominate.

In Palo Alto, I felt mature and appreciated. Perhaps it was so ideal because of the special program in which I got to deal directly with staff doctors, without a hierarchy of residents in between. I watched one greying paediatrician get down on the floor to play with one of his little patients. People were approached courteously, as the clinic was geared to the local community, unlike the only other multi-specialty practice at the time, the Mayo Clinic in Rochester, which focused on people from away.

At that point I didn't pay attention to funding models or comparisons to the system in Canada. I was only interested in soaking up as much medicine from these generous people as possible and in learning about their considerate treatment of fellow staff and patients, which I had never before witnessed in a hospital setting. I hardly remember the medical details, but I do recall their kindness and concern for other human beings.

We spent our weekends wandering up and down San Francisco streets, then driving back exhausted to Palo Alto on Sunday nights.

The weeks flew by. The Fiat continued to act up. With true diagnostic acumen, we finally figured it out: the car would always start within four hours, or in temperatures above 40 degrees Fahrenheit. Any longer, or any colder, meant she needed a boost. So, for the entire two months in California, the Fiat had to be started every four hours, more often if the temperature dropped. This entailed middle-of-the-night runs, until Jonathan was stopped by the cops at 4:30 am, for walking the streets in his pyjamas. We finally relented and used the few pennies we had saved to buy a new battery.

The Fiat ultimately delivered us safely back to Toronto. Along the way I had learned about automobiles, adversity, problem-solving and even about living together, much to my sister's dismay. Another lap of my medical education was complete and the journey had taught me as much as the destination.

CHAPTER 3

The Boss

'Clerkship', the final year of medical school, was divided into two-month blocks, or rotations, spent in different specialties in our home-based Toronto hospitals. All rotations were compulsory except one, which I had spent in California on my elective. As clerks, we became part of the hospital team involved in both in- and out-patient care, always assigned to the scut work, or dirty work, that more senior doctors felt was beneath them—getting up in the middle of the night to re-insert displaced intravenous lines, writing up long detailed notes on charts, seeing the drunks in the Emergency Department, walking to Medical Records to retrieve heavy files and cleaning up messes too unpleasant to describe. In addition, we shared the usual patient care responsibilities of doing histories and physical examinations, which were promptly re-done by our seniors, who then cross-examined us on every single finding.

One afternoon during my surgical rotation I decided to drop in on a young woman recovering from gall bladder removal the day before, at which I'd assisted. Miss Wilson's surgeon was a well-known stickler for detail so I wanted to be fully prepared for rounds the next morning. Grabbing her file from the nursing station, I headed down to her four-person room. I would have to address her as 'Miss Wilson' because we were taught that calling patients by their first names was disrespectful—one of the bizarre and seemingly nonsensical rules concerning patient care, with which I was still trying to come to terms.

I took a special interest in her. She was bright, 24 years old like me and she had an interesting history. She had already told me how she had bought her own little bungalow in the east end of the city and that she taught grade 4 in a public school nearby. She was always lively and inter-active with her students, but would suddenly have to race out of the classroom with abdominal pains to vomit. The pains persisted for several days and then mysteriously vanished, recurring several months later, unrelated to any foods she was eating. She was repeatedly told it was 'in her head' or due to 'her nerves' about teaching, even though her complaints continued into her third year at the same school.

It was only after seeing a female psychiatrist, who suggested she have her gall bladder checked, that Miss Wilson was sent for an oral cholecystogram, or an X-ray taken twelve hours after ingestion of a dye, which revealed multiple large gallstones. According to our teaching, this diagnosis was only made in females who were 'fat, flatulent and forty', none of which applied to her. Miss Wilson was then referred to the surgeon, Dr Fist, for cholecystectomy, or gall bladder resection, to be done through a large abdominal incision (unlike today, when it's done through a laparoscope inserted through tiny cuts in the belly).

Pulling the curtain around her bed for privacy, I began cheerfully. "Hi, Miss Wilson. How are you doing since your surgery?"

"Not too bad," she said slowly, "but I have some concerns I'd like to talk to you about."

"Go ahead. I hope I can help."

"I remember being wheeled into the operating room. I think I spoke to you just before that, didn't I?"

"Yes, we had a laugh in the hall because you recognized me in my ridiculous cap and mask."

"Well, after that I spoke to the anaesthetist, who was a lovely man. He gave me an injection and asked me to start counting. I got to five and I guess I drifted off." She fell silent. "Then... I don't know exactly, but sometime after I nodded off, I heard voices. At first, they sounded far away, then they got closer. People were chatting right over me. At first I thought I was hallucinating. But I understood that I'd be asleep all through the surgery. I wasn't asleep, but I couldn't move. Not a muscle."

"Maybe you were dreaming? Those anaesthetic drugs can have some pretty strange effects on our brains..."

"No. Please. There's more," she snapped. "I started thinking. *Okay, I've got to be calm and think this through.* Then I realized the lovely classical music I had fallen asleep to was gone and some god-awful rock 'n' roll was playing. *What'll I do?* I wondered. I thought maybe I could open my eyes, but just then I felt someone shut them on me. I tried to give whoever it was a hand signal but no. I couldn't move.

"Then I heard *beep-beep-beep* in time with my heart beat. And *thoop-poop, thoop-poop* which matched my breathing. It was so weird. I was terrified. But I didn't feel any pain… although there was some pressure in my belly."

"This doesn't sound right," I said. "You were supposed to be asleep."

"Asleep? Maybe in a nightmare. I *tried* to sleep, but I hate Bruce Springsteen and that's all I could hear. I thought if only they would turn it off, maybe I *could* sleep. Then someone with a gruff voice, it sounded like Dr Fist, started talking about his Easter weekend in Montreal. There I was trying to sleep and he was talking about restaurants."

I was flabbergasted. "This is terrible. Have you told anyone else about this?"

"I'm not finished telling you yet. I heard him ask for suction. *Why was he asking for suction? What were they sucking out of me?* I wondered if maybe I was bleeding to death. I started to think that my gall bladder attacks were better than lying on that bloody table aware of everything. Then suddenly he shouted, *She's not retracting hard enough. What's wrong with her?* And I heard this feeble female voice from across the room. *I'm feeling light-headed. I have to sit down…*"

"Oh my God! That was me!" Appalled by her tale, I jumped right in, "You heard the whole thing? You were alert, hearing and receiving everything?"

She nodded.

"We had no clue. I'm so sorry. This is so awful…" I practically fell over my words. I was shocked. "Did you ever fall back to sleep?"

"Eventually I did. But not before hearing the doctor swear about women not being strong enough to work with him. I smelled burning flesh. I had to work really hard trying to calm myself. Eventually I decided to beam the message from my hyper-active brain that I needed more drugs: *GIVE ME SOME DRUGS, PLEASE, SOMEONE…* And that's all I remember until I pried my eyes open in the recovery room and felt so nauseous I asked for Gravol. Do you remember?"

I nodded and we were both silent for a moment.

"What do we do now?" she asked.

"Tell Dr Fist what you told me. He needs to know."

"He's a pretty scary guy. Can you be with me when I tell him?"

I promised to accompany him on rounds in the morning and with the horror of her story flooding my brain, I rushed out of her room, heading straight for the library.

I worried about Dr Fist's reaction to her story. He was well-known as an arrogant perfectionist. I'd been warned about him before joining his service. I'd tried to get assigned to any other surgeon, but being 'low man on the totem pole', as we were called, I had no choice. I tried hard to please and stay out of trouble and, as we used to say, that's when Murphy's Law kicks in. Everything that can go wrong, will go wrong.

I'd studied the way he'd scrub his hands at the sink outside the operating room and tried to imitate his style exactly: scrubbing each finger and each side of every finger with the abrasive brush as many times as he did, until my hands were raw. But in my nervous state, inevitably on the way into the OR, my elbow would brush the door and he'd screech at me to re-scrub—a tough thing to do with tears of frustration further contaminating my hands.

I set myself up at a table in the library, grabbed a pile of anaesthetic and surgical textbooks and asked the librarian for help searching titles in journals over the previous twenty years—all that was currently available. Many hours later, we came up with nothing. I had no documented corroboration of Miss Wilson's story. But I still believed every word she said.

Exhausted and bewildered, I dragged myself down to the over-lit cafeteria for a late supper alone, then trudged up to my on-call room, set the alarm for 5 am to be sure I didn't sleep through rounds and fell into bed.

At 6:30 am, I joined the phalanx of white-coated doctors of all ages and sizes following the stocky man with closely cropped hair around the quiet halls. Thick tension prevailed as each of us awaited our individual grilling. The closer we got to Miss Wilson's room, the louder the thud in my chest.

Finally, we approached her bed, my hands shaking around her file.

"Good morning, Miss Wilson," I said, noticing how she appeared unexpectedly bright and calm. "Dr Fist, Miss Wilson has something she'd like to report."

"Go ahead," he said, facing her straight on, his forearms crossed over his chest. She slowly told her tale, her voice losing strength as her eyes welled up.

"You could have lightened a little… but this just doesn't happen. It was probably a dream you had as you went under."

"But I heard you talking about your plans to go to Montreal for Easter. And your assistant here became faint and had to sit down. And you know every single word to all of Bruce Springsteen's songs."

"Hmm," he cleared his throat. "Not to worry, your scar will heal beautifully and you can tell your dentist to give you a little extra anaesthetic the next time he puts you under," he said, quickly leaving the room.

Tearfully, the patient turned to me. All I could do was murmur, "I'm so sorry."

I followed Fist into the corridor, expecting him to explode at me. But he kept on walking down the hall, head held high, back rigid. Then turning suddenly, he grabbed a file. "Who's next?"

I wanted to chase after him with my questions, but fear got in my way. Instead, I slunk off to hide out in the doctor's lounge.

I washed my face, gently sprinkled cold water on my wrists and decided to do the best I could. I went back to Miss Wilson, listened to her feelings about the exchange with Fist and tried to reassure her. We discussed ways to avoid this happening again in the future. Walking away from her room, I realized that Fist didn't even blame the anaesthetist, or think to report it to him in order to prevent such an event from recurring. I flashed back on myself as a five-year-old being disregarded by the doctor. Yet, I also carried the injunctions from my family to not 'rock the boat' as was repeated to us: "*Fung Nisht Un.*" (Yiddish for don't start up.) So I learned to put up and shut up.

Today, a search of the literature entails typing *waking up in surgery* into Google and getting 4,750,000 references within .16 seconds. Anaesthesia Awareness or Intraoperative Awareness is a phenomenon not widely acknowledged before 2001.

One in one thousand patients every year wakes up during surgery. Brain active and receiving input, i.e. hearing, seeing, smelling, but paralyzed by anaesthetic drugs for output. Unable to move an index finger to indicate that something is wrong. Blood pressure may rise from the terror of receiving, without means of expression.

It occurs as a result of either insufficient anaesthetic being given in order to avoid excessive doses, or from inaccurate or inadequate monitoring of the patient's physical indicators. Years ago, people who complained about it were told they were wrong or crazy and half went on to develop symptoms of Post Traumatic Stress Disorder. Only now are newer devices being developed to monitor brain wave activity more closely to prevent this not uncommon event.

My surgical rotation represented my own awakening—I learned that doctors weren't perfect, that beneath the glamour of medicine was a whole lot of 'grist awaiting the mill'. I needed to learn to process and sort and accept that I could also make mistakes. To succeed, I'd have to juggle competing parties' interests while attempting to take care of myself, sometimes easily, and many times with great difficulty and frustration.

CHAPTER 4

"Peace Train"

My clerkship year drew to a close. The end of school was a relief, but thoughts of the final exams filled me with terror. If I passed the LMCCs (Licentiate of Medical Council of Canada), I would graduate and finally be granted the coveted MD degree.

The elation upon exiting the final exam was overwhelming. I was exhausted, dumbfounded, delighted. But soon fear set in: come July, I would be a real doctor and begin my internship. No excuse for mistakes. The full burden of error would be on my shoulders. I would be totally responsible and could lose the license I had worked so hard to get.

But first, I had one month to enjoy a holiday and rest. Jonathan and I had planned to celebrate by taking another road trip. This time in a sturdier car, across Canada and with company, my long-time friend Enid and her husband Earl. In May 1971, we set off for Vancouver in Earl's mother's white, finned Cadillac. Earl had done a lot of persuasive talking to encourage his mother to part with her brand new convertible. We promised to be back in a month for graduation. As we booted up to the 401 West, music blared. We laughed. Enid took charge of the maps in the front seat.

On the plush back seat, I fell asleep immediately. During that period of my life, whether it was Janice Joplin at top volume, Sha-Na-Na Live in concert, or a Truffaut movie, it all sent me into a deep sleep. This situation was no different. I had spent many late nights studying and on-call hours clerking, so I grabbed every opportunity for some shut-eye and shut-down of the brain. Each time I opened my eyes, I saw the 401, heard music and bantering and soon nodded off again.

I wondered if there was something wrong with me that I kept dozing off, while the others were wide awake. It didn't seem to be gender-related, as Enid was full of beans. There was a pressure to stay alert, to keep up with everyone else. I felt exactly as I did in medical school, where the fear of competition drove me to try harder. I didn't want to fall behind or act needy or 'girlie', so I ended up pushing myself even more. I was forced to hide my fatigue, my doubts, my questions, which I couldn't even admit to my mother. I didn't want to worry her. If she thought I was struggling, she would encourage me to take an easier route. I knew how much she cared for me and wanted me to be independent, but also wouldn't want it to be hard for me. I feared that admitting my difficulties, as I had to George Molen earlier on, would only lead to quitting and I no longer wanted to quit. I knew I could do it.

We made only the necessary stops along the way. I awakened briefly as we passed through the Sault. Later in Winnipeg, I dragged myself out of the car to eat and pee, then fell back onto the seat and dozed. That night we stayed in a cheesy, smelly motel room in Regina and then Enid drove across the prairies. As we pulled into Vancouver, I realized I'd slept all the way across Canada. All five days. I felt resentful that I was so exhausted, I had missed the whole trip. But I couldn't fight it. Those six years had taken their toll.

Earl had graduated two years earlier and had a bachelor classmate who was already working as an emergency physician at the Vancouver General Hospital. With a couple of other doctors, Darcy had rented a place, known as the 'party house' with lots of rooms for out-of-town guests. It looked exactly as expected: a two-storey back-split, with lush gardens and an enormous pool overlooking the ocean. Bikini-clad damsels, cold beer, stacks of empties, speakers blaring Cat Stevens' *Peace Train*.

Jonathan and I went to stay with Sidney, the family-friend who had lived across the street from my parents in Toronto— he of the 'painted fingernail' comment. I appeared as a proud soon-to-be doctor, proving his sexist theory wrong. He seemed to have forgotten his warning and was pleased to host us at his newly renovated home on Granville Street. He was now a successful urologist, who until recently had visited his parents in Toronto as a bachelor. But the home he welcomed us into was peopled by a wife and two children. He so feared his father's rage about marrying outside the faith that he lived a double life for many years until his father died, when he finally admitted it to his mother, who was delighted to discover she had grandchildren.

Enid and Earl stayed at Darcy's. We joined them to tour Simon Fraser University, take the ferry to Victoria with its predominantly blue-haired-lady population, wander around Vancouver viewing the hippies on Kitsilano Beach and mingle in the bead shops on West Fourth. We were on holiday, so didn't go near a hospital, but at Darcy's place we met several emergency docs from the Vancouver General Hospital—all tall, good-looking, very confident young men, but no women doctors. Darcy was twenty-six, appeared seventeen, cute and full of life. Away from his Toronto family, he was utilizing his hard-earned skills whilst frolicking in the temperate weather and loving his life.

The scene at Darcy's was right out of a television doctor series—hearty partying alongside serious workload. Watching those guys and hearing some of their hair-raising stories from the emergency department, I realized that medicine would always have huge ups and downs and enormous contrasts, like the law of physics studied early on:

For every action there is an equal and opposite reaction. The cost of freedom, satisfaction and money to burn was a lot of hard work, deep stress and endless drudgery.

I wasn't sure I was ready for an ongoing life of such vicissitudes. I'd believed that once I finished med school and got my degree, the tough stuff would be over, I'd be respected and could do my job and live my life. What I realized in Vancouver was that I had to seize the moment and appreciate the rewards and distractions in order to arm myself for whatever lay ahead.

I rested, slept and read a novel for the first time in six years. I quickly regained enough energy to party, splash in the pool and dance until 3 am. Then we had to jump back in the Caddy to blur our way across Canada in time for a very serious graduation ceremony.

My internship at North York General Hospital was pleasantly the opposite of what I had expected. I worked directly with staff doctors as I had in Palo Alto, without the intermediary hierarchy of residents. One of the obstetricians, with whom I worked well, jokingly called me *Buttercup,* inadvertently providing fellow interns with fodder enough to tease me for the remainder of the year. I received excellent teaching and felt seen and validated for the first time since Palo Alto. Confidence in my medical skills increased exponentially.

But the drawback to having no intermediary residents and few interns was that we each had frequent on-call duties— every second or third night—in order to adequately cover all services. The result was endless exhaustion all over again, so fatigued that during rare time off I slept through every movie I attended.

Jonathan and I moved into a tiny flat together in North Toronto. Although we rarely saw each other because of our workloads, we decided to get married half way through our internship in January 1972. The issue of taking my husband's surname arose, but I had always been Sharon Baltman, had graduated as such, and I didn't want another name just because I was getting married. For feminist reasons I couldn't imagine ever changing my name, so I didn't.

And of course, my traditional older sister, Rena, questioned my decision. "But Jonathan is such a nice guy…"

It turned out to be a very exciting time, yet shadowed by overwhelming fatigue.

One night on-call, I rested on the narrow bed in the small sterile room in the basement of the hospital, wishing I could turn off the telephone ringer and get some sleep. Around 3 am, a call came about a man in the Intensive Care Unit (ICU) experiencing ventricular fibrillation. Grabbing my shoes and lab coat with its pockets laden with stethoscope, reflex hammer, drug dosage cards and the *Washington Manual*, I raced upstairs, protocols for cardiac arrest running through my brain, simultaneously wishing he would revert to a normal heart rhythm before I got there.

I also tried to recall which staff man was on duty that night to determine whether I would have a pleasant learning experience, or a horror show of humiliation by some consultant at the other end of the phone not wanting to get his butt out of bed.

By the time I reached the bedside, I was definitely wide awake, putting the lie to the need for coffee—a bit of adrenaline went a long way. I examined the patient, managed his condition with the appropriate drug and settled us all down again for the night. The terror in anticipation of the event was often greater than the incident itself.

Other times, I was called by the nurses and dragged myself out of bed to re-start an IV that had fallen out, or to examine a patient whose condition had deteriorated overnight. But when not on duty, I managed to enjoy wonderful sleeps in that tiny bed.

The Emergency Room is the most filmed and watched chapter of medicine, probably because of the public's endless curiosity about it. There were certainly outrageous situations when I worked there. One night an ambulance brought in a man with a piece of his penis still trapped inside a vacuum cleaner. We had to carefully remove the piece and then store it in the freezer for possible grafting. While looking for a popsicle, one of the staff grabbed it by mistake. Another evening a man arrived with an onion stuck in his butt, being used as a stimulant and it had to be removed one layer at a time. Yet another night a man came rushing into emerg, pushing his elderly mother in her wheelchair, demanding she get immediate attention. The admitting nurse told me how she took one look at the patient and said, "Our doctor may be good, but she's not so talented that she can bring a dead person back to life." But such outlandish tales were rare in the usual routine of an emergency room.

When I worked there, I was usually the only doctor on duty, so I was constantly racing from one room to the next. The pace was rushed and unending, requiring on-the-spot flash decisions. One time, I was seeing a woman for a minor injury when I got called to see a man having a heart attack in the acute holding area. He had 'gone bad' quickly, triggering a Code 99, in which caregivers from all over the hospital converged with the Crash Cart to help out with the cardiac arrest. His breathing was obstructed. As the first one there, I struggled to put down an endotracheal tube to ventilate him, but couldn't get it in. When the anaesthetist arrived, she slid one in easily. I felt frustrated, but grateful for the assistance.

Another time I had to put in an intravenous line and poked someone several times without success, then the IV Team arrived and got it going quickly. It was exasperating for me, because I wasn't fulfilling the medical school adage of 'See one, Do one, Teach One'. Back then, because of such perfectionistic expectations, I remained focused on the negatives, the situations that didn't go well and it wasn't until years later that I learned to laud myself for the positives, the things I was doing right in my practice of medicine.

Overall, emergency work was interesting, exciting and challenging and could even be fun. I enjoyed the camaraderie of working as part of a team. The nurses and orderlies were available to deal with disruptive people, make suggestions, or just chat about shared, overwhelming experiences.

I was sad when attempts at reviving people were unsuccessful and then it was heart-wrenching to take the family into the quiet room to tell them they had just lost their loved one. I had worked hard to help save their relative and questioned myself. Had I done enough? Had I given the right drugs, too much, or not enough? In the midst of their sorrow and despair, I struggled with my doubts.

After a loss, I had no time to be frightened about seeing the next patient, as there was always someone waiting. Later, I tried to re-cap with co-workers, but there was never enough time. This residue collected in my brain and heart, to be dealt with later either consciously, or in my dreams.

The stress was cumulative, the excitement addictive.

Recently I read a book by Dr Frank Vertosick Jr., *When The Air Hits Your Brain*. Vertosick sounds like a pseudonym, but it is the real name of a Pennsylvania neurosurgeon, who is a good detail-man and an excellent teacher. Through his very clear descriptors included for the benefit of non-medical readers, I learned details about the functioning of the central nervous system that I had never understood from medical school.

He taught me that one part of the brain, the cerebellum, 'acts like a sculptor on an un-carved slab of marble, stripping away crass movements of another part of the brain, the cerebrum, to create refined finished products like muscle movements.' He claimed that his elegant, uncomplicated metaphors were gleaned from his own mentors.

His stories re-kindled some of those sleep-deprived moments from my clerkship and internship, periods I could barely recall because of fatigue. Such experiences have caused me to entirely agree with a recent court action calling hospital residents' prolonged work hours a violation of human rights.

Frank Vertosick's reminders of sleep-deprivation from being on-call and the stress of emergency work helped me better understand my own trajectory in medicine—how I later gave up emergency work because I found it difficult being the unfamiliar physician blamed for negative health outcomes by families. I preferred to develop ongoing relationships over years with patients in my own general practice office, so that after their tense moments in urgent care, I could step in as their empathetic GP. Looking for an even slower pace, I then moved to full-time psychotherapy, working only with people suffering chronic illnesses. But that was much later.

CHAPTER 5

Dr Frank

After working hard for seven years in medical school and internship, I needed to break out in a major way. Jonathan and I had travelled across Canada and the US, but I felt there was a whole world yet to be explored. I suggested that if we worked in an exotic locale, then we could keep our fingers in medicine and satisfy my travel bug at the same time. Jonathan was willing to go along. Most of our classmates were anxious to dive into one of the many high-paying general practice jobs available, or start their specialist training, settle down, buy a house and begin adult lives. They thought we were nuts.

With a rotating internship complete in June, I was qualified to work as a General Practitioner in the community. Our plan was to spend the summer doing locums—treating other doctors' patients in their offices while they were away on holiday or maternity leave.

Being out there on my own in the real world, outside the protective walls of the hospital, was a frightening prospect, but I knew my training had been good and if in doubt, I could ask questions of the boss or other physicians in the office. I could make a lot of money quickly, which I'd need for the next adventure, hopefully in October.

I searched locum ads in medical journals and at the Ontario Medical Association, but it was via word-of-mouth that I found Dr Frank Rayne and got an interview at his overflowing solo practice. It was my first trip to Scarborough, then commonly called Scarberia.

It was early morning when I pulled up in my blue Fiat hatchback to the address on Warden Avenue, just south of Lawrence, and parked outside a steel glass door at the end of a one-storey strip mall. The only other car in the lot was a big black Cadillac with the license plates *Dr Frank*. Not knowing what to expect, I nervously got out of my car, walked up to the glass door, pushed it open and entered a packed waiting room.

The receptionist was a nurse in full uniform of pressed white dress and starched cap with a black stripe. When I told her I'd come for an interview, she sent me down the hall to a small cubicle at the end. A big burly man was sitting at his desk, surrounded by shelves with hundreds of large labelled pill bottles of all colours and shapes.

"Frank Rayne," he said, extending his hand. "I'll pay you fifty per cent of the take and don't forget to keep your own list of patients. Just to keep me honest. Ready to start?"

Turning away, he began counting tablets into a bottle. "But I'm here for an interview," I stammered.

"No need for that. Grab a lab-coat and stethoscope, step across the hall and go to it."

"But I have another interview later this morning."

"Don't worry about that. I'll keep you busy. Now you don't want to disappoint those patients out there, do you? They've been waiting a long time to see a fine lady doctor just like you."

I was confused. He barely knew my name yet he was offering me a chance to practise medicine in his office without checking my references, credentials or even my ID, unthinkable in any sector today. He was counting out pills, yet I'd been taught that patients took a prescription to the local pharmacy for medication, as physicians didn't have a license to dispense their own drugs.

But in those days, I was still pretty daunted by men, in spite of my attempts to be their equal. I had grown up in a house where my mother was a homemaker, always lovingly available to her children as well as to her husband, whose every need she doted upon. Although Hellie encouraged my independence, her role-model was that of caregiver. Her mother, my grandmother *Bubby* Nancy, catered to her husband until he was 97 years old. So male directives were pretty powerful for me. Besides, Dr Frank was paying and I needed a job.

My first patient was a young kid with a sore throat. There was no obvious evidence of infection, so I asked the nurse for a throat swab. Laughing, she said Dr Frank never bothered with those. He just gave them all a bottle of penicillin.

"I see," I mumbled, not seeing anything but my own doubts. I meekly suggested to Dr Frank that I'd rather write a prescription for a patient to fill at the drugstore, as we were taught to do.

"Don't be ridiculous. You tell me what they need and I'll fix them right up with pills now and I'll show you the ropes later when you're done."

An anxious housewife wanted Valium. He popped some into a bottle and handed it to her. A young girl had a urinary tract infection so he counted out sulpha tablets. And so the morning continued. As noon approached, the waiting room was fuller than when I'd arrived. I hadn't even made a dent in the crowd, but I was determined to get to my other interview.

Big smile from Frank when I told him I was leaving.

"See you tomorrow at nine. Be prepared to stay late. Tuesday's my long day. Good work, Sharon."

And out I flew. I could hardly get my keys out of my purse and into the ignition as my hands were shaking. I pulled away from the strip-mall, thinking I never wanted to return. I didn't like Frank handing out drugs to the patients I was seeing. I didn't have a license to dispense and I didn't know whether he did. Could I lose my medical license over this?

As I drove to the interview at the other doctors' office, I calmed myself by deciding that I'd take any other job offered. I was afraid to work with Dr Frank.

I arrived at a large family practice office downtown. The woman at the desk took my name, ran into the back and quickly returned, saying that after checking with her boss, there must be some mistake. The clinic needed a 'man-doctor'.

Early next morning I returned to the Scarborough parking lot. More calmly than the day before, I pushed open the heavy glass door, finding several patients already ensconced. This time I noticed an ugly landscape painting that adorned the wall over their heads—jagged mountain ranges against a clear blue sky. My father had one of those over a grungy stairwell at *the shop* on Dundas Street East—a freebie with gas purchase years ago.

I saw patients and Frank handed out the meds I recommended. And so it continued for the next week.

One morning I arrived to discover from nurse Lucy that Dr Frank wouldn't be in until later. I'd have to hand out the medications myself. I protested that I didn't have a license to dispense, so it would be illegal for me to do so and instead I would write prescriptions the patients could fill at the local pharmacy. She told me the doctor would hit the roof if I did that, quietly admitting that he made a 'pretty penny' doing this on the side. She explained that because he had a dispensing license from working up north, I could also dispense out of his office. An easy-going woman in her fifties, Lucy had worked with Dr Frank for years in North Bay. Clearly, she was trying hard to keep things together in the office. She handled the patients well, having a warm connection with most of them.

Suddenly, the long hours on call at the hospital seemed easy. Medical school hadn't prepared me with crib sheets or how-to lessons for dealing with other doctors.

I picked up my tools, called in a patient and went to work. More of the same illnesses, but now I also had to rummage around in the dispensary, find the appropriate meds, count them into a container and stick on a label.

That wasn't so hard, I thought. It was exactly what the pharmacist would have done. Asking Lucy for reassurance that my first bottles were done correctly, I handed out only what was absolutely essential. Still, thoughts plagued me. Did Frank really have a license to dispense? Would I get into trouble for following suit?

In med school, we were warned about antibiotic-resistant bacteria. Because antibiotics were being prescribed so frequently since their discovery thirty years earlier, the bugs they were aimed at were mutating, changing their structures, so they were no longer susceptible to the original drug. These 'superbugs' needed newer and stronger compounds to kill them off—a boon to the pharmaceutical industry, but a bust for patients requiring more potent and more expensive treatments.

First determining the type of infection by taking throat swabs, I tried to avoid such over-use of antibiotics. The drug companies, pharmacies and Dr Frank would not be happy with me, but I stood my ground and handed out less penicillin than he would have liked.

My work became pretty routine over the next couple of weeks. I was still nervous about the dispensing issue, but was only planning to be there for three months. Time seemed to pass extremely slowly.

One day, just as I was beginning to do a pelvic examination on a young woman, my concentration was interrupted by loud bangings in the next room.

"I don't care if she can't see all the patients. I'm not feeling well, damn it!" a voice boomed through the paper-thin walls.

"Shsh, Frank, the patients will hear," whispered Lucy, none too quietly.

I wondered what was going on just as my patient asked: "There's quite a ruckus out there. It's not Dr Rayne again, is it?"

"What do you mean *again?*" I asked.

"This happened the last time I was here. That's why I told Lucy I would never come back, unless I could see a different doctor."

I quickly finished the woman's Pap smear, wrapping the elastic around the requisition, motioning for her to climb down off the examining table and get dressed.

"Very happy to meet you," she said. "I'll only come back if *you* are here next time. What's your name again?"

"Dr Baltman," I answered, wondering if *I* would be there next time.

"Well, thank you, Dr Baldwin," she said and went happily out the door.

I headed towards the voices emanating from the washroom at the back.

"I'm okay, for god's sake. It's *you* that has the problem," Dr Frank's voice roared. Through the open door, I saw him—hair askew, wobbling, eyes wet and red. The smell of alcohol hit me.

"Morning, Dr B. How are you? Hope you're ready for a big day. Lucy just convinced me to go home. I'll leave you to care for these darlings and I trust you to hand out lots of meds," he garbled.

"I'm happy to see and treat your patients, but I'm not licensed to hand out medications. I'll send them off to the local pharmacy with a prescription," I replied.

"Just count out the damn pills, would ya?" he barked.

"Sorry, I'm not able to see your patients unless I send them out for meds," I managed to say.

"Do what you want, but I gotta leave," he mumbled, wavering down the hall. Following him, I watched as he plunged out the front door, fell into his Cadillac and screeched away. I was shaking. I half-smiled to the witnessing patients, saying something about seeing them shortly. I wandered into one of the empty examining rooms and paced back and forth.

I started to put the pieces together—his rush for me to see people, his preferring to hide out in the back, his frequent absences. I was astonished and furious. I had no idea what to do, aside from seeing those poor people out front. Here was an older physician, whom I was taught to respect, showing up totally drunk. An alcoholic, who needed propping up. Instead of receiving mentoring and support in my first job, I was giving it. And after all those months of taking crap from my seniors in hospital, here it was happening outside. I was again caught in the middle between patients and another physician, as I had been with Dr Fist and his patient. At least in the heat of the moment I had stood up to Dr Frank about the prescribing issue.

But what about his unprofessional conduct? Reporting another physician for bad behaviour, sexual or otherwise was just not done then. And if I reported him, would I get into trouble? After all, I was the newbie and a girl, so how could I possibly have any credibility reporting a guy with twenty-five years' experience in solo general practice? Ethically and morally, he was wrong. But in the short-term, I had to find a solution to take care of the patients, take care of myself and keep everyone safe.

I continued to work in his practice, but without dispensing. Every morning I assessed Herr Doktor's aroma and his behaviour to guess his blood alcohol level and therefore his fitness to practise. If necessary, I sent him home by threatening to quit if he didn't leave. As long as I was there, I became the acting policewoman.

On the days he was sober, I could see what a nice guy he was—kind to his patients, gentle and understanding. I realized why he had such a loyal following. He was quite charming with Lucy and they seemed to have a good working relationship. Until he got into his bottles. Suddenly all the drinking and partying I witnessed with the Vancouver doctors took on a more sinister tone.

As my departure date approached, I worried about leaving Dr Frank's patients. They had gotten accustomed to heading out to the pharmacy and being seen regularly. What would happen when I left? I kept reminding him I was leaving, asking if he'd made plans to replace me. He repeated that he'd worry about it when the time came.

Once again I decided to take matters into my own hands by asking colleagues if anyone was interested in assuming a locum position. A former classmate, Gail, contacted me and we arranged to meet at the office. She was a hard worker, wouldn't be pushed around and was also able to joke with a deep hearty laugh. But because of her small stature, I worried that Dr Frank would take advantage of her.

"I want to be perfectly clear with you. The practice is great—lots of lovely patients, interesting pathology, well-paid. But the job entails some extra-curricular duties."

"And what might those be?" Gail asked suspiciously.

"Not what you're thinking. He's an alcoholic. So the first thing you do when he arrives is assess his fitness to practise. If he's inebriated, send him home. Secondly, don't let him hoodwink you into handing out drugs. He's got a license to dispense from working up north. We don't. Don't put yourself at risk to make him some money, or to please him. Thirdly, make sure you pass this advice on to the locum who replaces you."

"That's a lot to deal with. But I need the work. Thanks for warning me."

"No problem. Are you ready to meet him? He's actually quite sober today," I whispered, leading her down the hall to the big boss.

"Dr Rayne, this is Gail, the doctor I was telling you about. She's agreed to take over for me," I said. "I've got to run. Good luck."

Grabbing my purse, I rushed out the steel glass door for the last time, past the black Cadillac and headed off to get a Yellow Fever shot. Having learned to say no to a senior colleague, I already possessed the other immunity which would serve me well in my upcoming African experience.

CHAPTER 6

Accra, Accra, Accra

How did four newly-minted doctors with traditional Jewish backgrounds end up getting jobs in a Catholic Medical Mission hospital in Ghana, West Africa? I certainly have no idea, aside from the fact that Jonathan and I, and our old travel buddies, Enid and Earl, were seeking adventure as medical volunteers in what was then called a third world country.

Global travel was unusual then and communication very difficult. Letters from home could only be received 'Care of Poste Restante' at the central post office in major cities and could take weeks or months to arrive. Phoning was very complicated. So our plan to live in Africa for two months and then travel for another six would definitely result in very little contact with our families back home.

If my family was apprehensive about my going, they didn't let on. Over the years, they had witnessed my perseverance despite objections, in attending medical school, travelling with my boyfriend in Europe and then living with him before marriage. When we did get married, we had a small, non-traditional wedding with only immediate family and friends. So by the time I was planning to go to Africa, my relatives had learned that once I made up my mind there was no point trying to object—there would be no stopping me.

This didn't mean I was indifferent about leaving. I cried my eyes out saying good-byes at the airport to my mother and younger sister Lynni, only thirteen at the time. I then met the other three at the gate and we boarded the plane to New York City, from there catching an eight-hour overnight flight to Casablanca. Half-asleep and disoriented, we changed planes there to venture deeper into Africa. On the roof of the building, silhouetted against the dawning light, stood dark, burqa-clad figures, their ululating piercing the crispy air.

The next thing I knew, we were landing in Accra, the capital of Ghana. The door of the plane opened and I stepped into a wall of heat and humidity. The airport was jammed with bodies rushing the gates to greet loved ones in the arrival lounge. Amid the chaos I eventually retrieved my bags and picking one of the many drivers yelling, "Accra Accra Accra," the four of us scrambled into a car and headed downtown to a recommended guest house.

The streets were filled with people racing in all directions. Women in dark-patterned, two-piece, full-length dresses with huge loads balanced on their heads. Constant honking. No sidewalks and no stoplights.

Later, we went for a walk in the blaring sunshine. I felt we were in Makola market long before we reached it. Our white faces flashed like blinking signs as little ones ran up to touch us and feel our pale skin, not asking for 'baksheesh' or alms, as kids learned to do years later.

"*Yavu, Yavu...*" they called after us. I did not yet recognize the term Ghanaians used for the original missionaries in their country, which meant 'white man with black beard'. *Yavu* now signified any white foreigner. At the side of the road, women sat tending large round metal buckets of fire, cooking slices of plantain and skewers of meat. Babies tied in printed fabric were slung on mothers' backs and barefoot toddlers ran around carrying smaller ones on their tiny torsos. People were welcoming and constantly offered help. Taxi drivers and 'Mammy' bus drivers repeatedly shouted strange place names.

We spent three days wandering the city, discovering the enormous British-built post office, touring the American-built hospital, then finally contacting the Mission people. Every little chore in Accra took forever. To brush my teeth I had to first boil water; to make a local call entailed a trip to the post office where the phones functioned inconsistently. Frustrated missionaries later taught us the expression: 'WAWA', which meant 'West Africa Wins Again'.

The fourth day brought a bumpy, dusty bus ride to Kpandu. Stumbling off with our gear, the four of us were left beside the road, standing on a sandy spot next to a crudely-dug ditch. Thick trees rose overhead. Women in long dresses with heavy stacks of fruit and wood perched on their heads ambled by, a slow-motion version of Accra. Suddenly, a tall black man in Western dress approached us from a van parked under a tree.

"Honoured to meet you, my dear friends. Welcome to Kpandu. I am Benjamin Owabi. I work at the hospital. Please, come. I will drive you." He shook the men's hands and nodded to Enid and me to jump on board. We bumped along in silence, peering out at the ever-narrowing corrugated road. As we journeyed deeper into the unknown, I worried less about creature comforts and more about tropical diseases so easily transmitted via contaminated water, food, insects and air droplets. I had been warned not to drink or eat anything unless it was boiled or peeled.

In the midst of my reverie, Mr Owabi stopped the truck, announcing our arrival at the compound, a cluster of bunker-like concrete buildings in a clearing between the trees. He led the way, showing us into a big sparse room where we were greeted by a tall, skinny, straight-standing, grey-haired lady wearing a faded blue house-dress. She did not look healthy. Pale, fidgety, but commanding and precise, she was probably in her mid-forties but looked sixty.

"Yoh, it is nice to get some help viss my verk. Wilkommen. I am Dr Marquart. Pleeze, trink some wasser, my greeting to you."

Water is the greeting in West Africa, but Dr M. said nothing about this water being safe to drink. Searching for clues from Earl who was studying internal medicine, I saw him raise the glass to his mouth, but in spite of my thirsty, hot state, I barely let the water touch my lips.

Dr M. talked about how she had come from Germany fourteen years earlier to set up the hospital. Her nursing staff had come and gone but she had stayed even though she was nearly blind—with only tunnel vision remaining—from all the chloroquine medication she'd taken to treat malaria. She droned on about the hospital activities, elaborating on the schedule for rounds and how the generators worked only from 8 until 10 pm so she could save money on electricity.

After what felt like hours of lecturing, each couple was shown to a large room with a double canopy bed surrounded by a mosquito net. I hadn't noticed mosquitoes while listening to the briefing, but had caught sight of seven-inch praying mantises, green geckoes, bats and tarantulas the size of my palm. None of the windows had screens, hence the coverall mosquito nets. There was a sink in the corner of the room, with a pail on the floor next to it. They explained that because the lights and water only worked for two hours in the evening, the bucket needed to be filled the night before for wash-water the next morning. And there was no air conditioning, even though it was forty degrees in the cool breeze of evening.

We settled into the barren room and I flopped into bed, exhausted, uncertainties about this adventure swimming wildly in my brain. All I wanted to do was see the world, volunteer and practise medicine. But it was not turning out that simple.

I awoke next morning somewhat refreshed and ready to face whatever the day held for me. We went to the dining room for breakfast at 6:30 where we met fresh-faced, blonde nurses in crisp white uniforms gathered around the table. They spoke German with little English. Dr Marquart barely nodded as we slid into our seats. Placed before me was ground nut paste with stale bread and coffee. I hate peanut butter, so I downed black coffee with lots of sugar and choked down some dry bread.

Rounds began at 7 am sharp. Dr M. led us through the hospital compound along covered concrete walkways open to the heat on the sides, ending in several long, low-rise buildings. The wards consisted of two endless rows of beds jammed with patients with malaria, hepatitis, liver cancer, snakebites and gonococcal urethral strictures. Others had dehydration from salmonella or typhus. One child suffered from fulminating tuberculosis. People with untreated blood pressures so high, their kidneys had failed. I saw men with tropical parasites, like filariasis and hookworm. The soft-spoken patients asked few questions and were grateful for any small amount of attention paid to them. The nurses followed Dr M. around, doting on every word.

Many patients had complicated infections, which Dr Marquart treated with chloramphenicol, the only antibiotic she could obtain free from Germany. Earl immediately retorted that it can cause agranulocytosis, or destruction of all the blood cells. It terrified me to think of using such a dangerous medication. It was also frightening, yet fascinating, to see the illnesses I'd been warned about avoiding during travel, the ones that I, like Dr M., could easily contract. My head was spinning from all the diseases—an entire textbook of pathology before my eyes.

At the end of rounds, we followed Dr Marquart to the out-patient clinic. We walked by lines of patients stretched down the hall and around the corner onto the adjacent walkway. Families standing around, women sitting on the floor with crying babies, old, sunken-eyed men pacing, groups of teenage girls giggling. All turned to watch us march past. With people waiting patiently, Dr M. set herself up at a small school-desk at the head of the column and began her routine:

"A charama? A fojidama?" (Are you vomiting? Do you have diarrhoea?)

Physical examinations were conducted with the patient seated in full view of the line-up. It was vague at best. The most she could possibly do was look in the eyes for jaundice or anaemia, peer into the ears or throat for infection, note the colour and texture of the skin for dehydration and guess the amount of weight loss.

"Next."

Dr M. managed to make her way through tens of patients within three hours, clearing the lines by 2 pm, when she silently led the way back to the dining room for lunch.

After devouring a few bites of the same dry bread from breakfast, I headed back to my room without waiting for the others to decide what they wanted to do. The thought of a few minutes of shut-eye under the suffocating mosquito net kept me going. I grabbed a dollop of melted chocolate from my bag and burrowed under the net into my cocoon.

What a day! I suddenly realized how big a job I had taken on. I was overwhelmed by the severity of the illnesses, by the volumes of work, by the hot sticky weather, by the gentleness of the people. They never demanded anything, accepted whatever was offered and always responded with a smile.

I saw entire families sitting around a relative's bed together, eating a meal they had brought in. Little kids running quietly up and down the aisles between the beds in the infirmary.

Dr M's handling of patients was a shock. So different from medicine in Canada, where people could undress in a private room and be fully examined by the doctor. Where the 'Semmelweis' technique of handwashing between patients to prevent transmission of infection had been ground into our brains. Here, there was neither time nor facility for any of that.

I slept all afternoon until dinner at 6:30, which yielded bread, ground nut paste, *po-po* (local papaya) and corn-on-the-cob. This corn was not yummy Ontario peaches-and-cream corn, but had huge yellow kernels far apart and tasteless. In Canada it's called 'feed corn' supplied only to livestock. Fearing the corn, I again ate only dry bread and *po-po*. And so ended my introductory day to life in Kpandu. My mother had taught me that if you set your sights on doing something, you can accomplish it, even if it's difficult. Well, I was beginning to lose that belief.

From then on, Dr M. announced we would take turns either being on rounds with her, or working the clinic. My first week was to be spent in the clinic. Like the day before with Dr M., I walked in, sat down at the desk at the head of the line and began:

"*A charama? A fojidama?*"—the only questions I knew in the local language, Ewe.

At first, I felt I didn't know what I was doing. The nurses helped me get more information by holding the babies so moms could gesture to me. I passed out boxes of malaria pills to those with symptoms, I sent the sickest ones for admission to hospital, I gave eye and ear drops for infections and I used the dreaded chloramphenicol. For gastroenteritis, transmitted from one baby to the next by flies landing on their faces, there was little I could do aside from encouraging more breast feeding. Compared to the quality of care in Canada, my work seemed totally inadequate, but soon I realized I was providing valuable triage or sorting, so I settled into a rhythm, feeling I was indeed being helpful.

Until Dr Marquart arrived from rounds. Walking in, she sat down at the next desk and began vetoing my orders. When I suggested chloramphenicol, she refused it. When I withheld it, she gave it out. She pushed me to work faster, yet slowed down the line by interfering with my decisions. I felt totally frustrated. There was no way to please this woman. I had arrived keen, full of knowledge and experience from internship and practice in modern Toronto. She was telling me I knew nothing and every treatment plan was nixed. I worked robot-like, waiting for my orders to be switched.

During that week in the clinic, I gradually got more comfortable with the patients. I started to interact in sign language with them. I complimented a young girl's corn rows and she beamed. When I pointed to a woman's basket and nodded and raised my eyebrows, she tried to gift the bag to me. I rubbed an ill baby's soft tummy and the mom smiled. The smallest gesture was reciprocated ten times over. These people were quickly finding a way into my heart. But as soon as Dr M. arrived, the patients and I became serious and business-like.

"A charama? A fojidama?"

The following week, spending so much time on rounds with Dr M. was brutal. I learned a lot about how different diseases devastated the human body but I was constantly tense being with her. I couldn't answer her questions when she grilled me and I was terrified to express my opinion lest it differ from hers.

She also took me on rounds in private rooms, where several missionary priests had been brought to the hospital in very dire condition, seeking treatment of tropical diseases like malaria and amoebiasis acquired from their long-standing work abroad. They were expatriates who refused to go home for care because they felt Africa was 'home'. They talked critically about the local shamanic ritual of cutting the skin to 'release the devil' in order to cure illness. Throughout the wards I saw the scars of such cutting, many thickened keloids on chests, abdomens and faces of adults and tiny infants who were first treated locally by the shaman or medicine man before being brought to the clinic in desperation. The missionaries talked about how they had spent their whole lives trying to convert these people to Catholicism and western ways of healing. Thankfully the Catholic issue was not imposed upon us. We experienced Grace before meals and other blessing rituals but were not expected to go to church or to do any proselytizing.

Looking back on it, I can see that Dr M. had many years of experience in these conditions with this population and their ailments. I was arriving from a different planet with very cushy modern facilities. I didn't understand her side of the story which she certainly made no effort to explain and never responded when asked. I therefore had to suffer my way through, feeling deflated and discouraged. I had thoughts of quitting but couldn't imagine a way to get out. I had made a commitment with the Mission Board for two months and was determined to follow through. I had also agreed to spend that time with Jonathan in Africa, but more awkwardly, we as a couple had committed to being there with Enid and Earl. It was a joint venture.

The work was a grind and without edible meals, I had to find other ways to sustain myself. The four of us got together in the evenings after dinner. I tried to laugh, played chess and card games with the others. Enid and Earl were good company, always joking about something, often gallows humour about our situation. Dr M. forbade us to leave the compound in the dark, so we would sneak out by bicycle, motorbike or on foot to reach the local pub and score an ice-cold Pepsi-Cola.

One weekend a driver came to show us around Kpandu and there we met the only other white folks around—teachers with CUSO, Bill and Jane Campbell.

"We're here for a good time, not for a long time," Bill repeated endlessly. Every weekend, they picked us up in their car to drive all around Ghana, each time in a different direction. We toured around Lake Volta, then west to Kumasi to see the dam being built, supervised by expatriates. They drove us to Accra to see local bands playing 'high life' music in crowded clubs.

Bill and Jane's diet was more appealing as they were buying and cooking for themselves, thereby getting familiar with markets and vendors and learning about safer cuts of meat and how to bargain for them. They were immersed in the culture, which I missed, feeling cut off and isolated within the compound, unable to enjoy the locals because of Dr M's restrictions. It was like I had caught her tunnel vision—I was so busy trying to survive the ascetic conditions that I couldn't appreciate my surroundings.

I focused a great deal of my unhappiness on the lack of creature comforts, but that was the superficial issue. The real problem was the foreign nature of this practice of medicine— so primitive, so many gravely-ill patients, such a lack of facilities and medications for proper treatment. So different from the medicine that had surrounded me day and night for seven years.

Ironically, I was no longer afraid of getting sick. I'd done everything possible before the trip to keep myself safe—injections of gamma globulin to prevent hepatitis, shots against cholera, yellow fever, typhoid, tetanus-polio and the bitter chloroquine swallowed every Saturday for malaria prevention. And although none of these measures guaranteed a clean slate, I felt confident about my own health. But the medicine I was practising was so alien that I needed to fantasize about something familiar like a cold Pepsi, shipments of chocolate or new novels from home in order to stay grounded in that milieu whilst biding my time until the two months were over.

For my third week I was to be Dr M's surgical assistant, to 'be her eyes'. Early one morning she called me over before rounds to say we had to do a caesarean section. I marched quickly behind her into an empty room—in darkness—other than bits of light streaking in from small windows up high. The nurses wheeled in a pregnant woman on a gurney and positioned her under the modern operating room lights, which were off because the generator would not come on until later in the evening.

Dr M. scrubbed. I followed. The nurses opened a sterile tray and we gowned and gloved. As the patient writhed with contractions, we attempted to place sterile cloths around her belly where the incision would be, then swabbed her with brown antiseptic solution to cleanse the area. Dr M. fumbled for the scalpel.

"Aren't you going to inject some local anaesthetic?" I choked out.

Throwing the scalpel back onto the tray, she drew some xylocaine into a syringe. Scowling at me, she poked the squirming woman in two spots. The woman yelped.

"Happy now?" she asked, plunging the scalpel into the woman's belly. I couldn't see for blood, trying to sponge the red from the incision. The rest was a blur: the woman screaming, Dr Marquart snapping at me to clear the blood, darkness over the table, and finally the choking newborn. Dr M. quickly stitched her up until the bleeding stopped and we emerged into the sunlight of the corridor.

She wanted me to follow her to rounds, but I said I wasn't feeling well and had to go back to my room. I realized I was learning how *not* to practise medicine. I was solidifying my beliefs in the need to treat patients with consideration and understanding. And the way I was being treated reminded me of Dr Fist—nothing was good enough for the senior physician. Instead of patiently and helpfully instructing, they demanded and reprimanded, which only made me feel more useless and more tense. So it really didn't matter where I was, or what the conditions were, I would have to find ways to deal with other physicians. This time I would simply hang on until the ride was over.

After a month of this routine, I was bush-whacked, losing weight, protein-deficient and feeling awful. I was having a hard time writing cheery letters home, trying to convince my family not to worry and that all was well when it wasn't. I had a lot of interesting stories to tell, but I was exhausted.

In the fifth week, Koos appeared. A Dutch doctor from the neighbouring Catholic Medical Mission in Dzodze, close to the border with Togo. He needed help and asked if Dr M. could possibly spare one of the doctor-couples. I immediately volunteered, using the new skill of speaking up I had learned with Dr Frank.

Arriving in Dzodze was like coming home. Jonathan and I had a bedroom with adjacent bathroom, a shower spewing hot water twenty-four hours a day. There was a large, cosy living/dining room with pictures on the wall and comfy couches. The kitchen was enormous, with well-stocked cupboards and a full refrigerator.

I wandered around the rooms inspecting the screens on all the windows, feeling the breeze blow in, bugs filtered out. I would no longer be prey for malaria-laden mosquitoes and dysentery-carrying flies twenty-four hours a day. I wouldn't have to sleep under an oppressive mosquito net to protect myself overnight. Here, the generators worked night and day. Life suddenly looked familiar in this Dutch home in the middle of Ghana.

After offering us a plate of familiar crusty French bread and butter, Koos's lovely wife, Marjanne, broke a bar of chocolate into pieces on a plate.

Koos joked: "We may be missionaries in Africa, but we need a little bit of Holland with us."

The next day, Jonathan and I followed Koos on his rounds, discussed cases with him. Our input was welcomed. I saw many people and a multitude of fascinating diseases, but patients weren't herded around a factory like in Kpandu and their privacy was respected. The hospital resembled ones back home. I finally got to laugh and joke with people, truly enjoying the doctor-patient interactions and never had to use chloramphenicol.

"I don't use that *godverdomme* (God-damn) stuff," Koos laughed. "I get shipments of penicillin, ampicillin and even Bactrim from home."

I met their cheerful young housekeeper, Millicent Mercy Dome, who insisted upon sewing a local outfit for me. She dragged me off to the market to search for the perfect cotton, a quiet print in yellow and green. She measured me and disappeared, returning a few days later with a short-sleeve blouse ruffled around the neck with a matching full-length pencil skirt. Although I could walk only in very short baby-steps, she assured me it fit perfectly.

After two weeks in Dzodze, images of Kpandu began to fade. I had twinges of guilt about having left Enid and Earl behind, but I quickly rationalized that they could look after themselves. We had planned to meet up again in Accra at the end of the second month to continue our travels together, when I would pretend that our experience in Dzodze had not been staggeringly different. I would not let on that by speaking up when Koos arrived, I had forced a change, proving that the Kpandu situation was not about Africa or Ghana or Mission Hospitals. It was about the person in charge, the CEO.

While Dr Marquart was arrogant, rigid and demanding, making for an intolerable situation, Koos was humble, flexible and open, had a sense of humour and created a marvellous learning environment. And West Africa did *not* Win Again, because I managed *not* to contract any tropical disease in spite of the conditions the first month.

Thirty-five years later, I still have my Ghanaian outfit hanging in my basement as a memento. Global travel is more ubiquitous now and a few years ago my daughter went to Africa and fell in love with Ghana and its people, as I had. Her descriptions and photos of the roads and villages and houses closely resemble what I saw back then. Entirely coincidentally, she visited Kpandu, but missed seeing the hospital, which had been re-named the Margret Marquart Catholic Hospital.

Dr M. clearly left a very different impression on her superiors in the Catholic Church than she did on me. Even *Stern Magazine* wrote that 'she was the *ungewöhnlichste* (most unusual) woman that Ghana ever knew'.

CHAPTER 7

Szabo and Jones

With the completion of our assignment in Ghana, the hard work of our trip was not over. We had yet to embark on the travel and leisure portion, which I hadn't realized would also be labour-intensive, especially on a limited budget in the early '70s and to the countries we planned to visit. Flying to Nairobi, I wondered what East Africa had in store.

The answer arrived on a busy Western-style street in the capital city of Kenya, in broad daylight, with a man trying to grab my purse. I managed to wrestle it back from him, but was left shocked and shaken. In spite of the upset, I remained determined to carry on with our plans to greet the New Year 1973 on the east coast in Mombasa. We secured the last two hotel rooms available on the beach on New Year's Eve.

Jonathan and I had been travelling with Enid and Earl on and off since October. My idea of touring was the slow, delicious exploration of each site, but Earl's style was to stop just long enough to take pictures and then hurry off to the next attraction. In the beach-front hotel room, where the shower spewed only salt water and we slept under yet another mosquito net, I decided I wanted us to separate from the other couple. Jon was reluctant, but eventually concurred. We agreed to continue together through the countries where travelling in a group would be cheaper and possibly safer, like Africa, India and Nepal, but thereafter, the couples would go their separate ways in South-East Asia.

The following week, quite amicably, all four of us headed out to tour the game parks in Ngorongoro Crater in Tanzania. Earl was at the wheel of our rented Land Rover when we were suddenly faced with a herd of elephants. Cursing loudly, Earl could not find first gear. So there we sat with elephants sniffing around our car. What felt like hours later, Earl suddenly jerked us into forward gear and slowly inched us through them.

The next week we flew to Ethiopia, where we visited the village of Woleka in which the Felashas, a lost tribe of Judah, lived in domed mud huts, practising an ancient form of Judaism. I spoke to them in Hebrew, which they said was the language they studied at school. Inside the mud synagogue, the children sang *Hayvainu Shalom Aleichem* (Welcome and Peace Be With You). The teacher told me they had very few Hebrew prayer books and I offered to ask my mother to ship some. Years later, in the drought of 1991, the entire tribe was air-lifted to Israel, the homeland of their dreams, so that currently only one elderly woman remains in the village, refusing to leave her life-long home.

From Ethiopia, we flew to Bombay (now Mumbai). Our first Indian train ride to visit the caves of Aurangabad was crammed with wall-to-wall people and chickens and goats, so we decided thereafter to take full advantage of our round-the-world airline tickets and fly from city to city within India—from Udaipur to Jaipur with its pink palace, to the chaos of Delhi, where we were driven around in rickshaws through crowded, noisy streets. During three weeks in India, going from the Taj Mahal to cremations on the Ganges, we were overwhelmed by the crowds but never stopped moving ourselves. From there to Katmandu, Nepal, where the four of us arranged to go trekking in the Himalayas, guided by Sherpas—one exquisite week of sleeping in tents on the sides of mountains and getting stoned on hashish we'd legally purchased in a store on the main street in town.

After two more months of travel together, upon returning to Katmandu, the two couples separated as planned. Jonathan was not pleased to go off on our own, preferring the security and cost-splitting provided by the other two. But he and I talked it through using what I thought of as our fine skills at compromise. A sinus infection that we treated with one of the trusty antibiotics brought from home kept me in bed for two weeks in Katmandu, but once it settled, I was raring to go.

Jonathan and I took off on our own. We explored Thailand, Malaysia, Singapore and then on to Indonesia, viewing the artwork in Jogjakarta, then flying to heavenly Bali, where I wanted to hang out on Kuta Beach for as long as possible. Nightly, we feasted cheaply on 'Chicken Delicious' or lobster, followed by yummy hash brownies. The town had narrow dirt roads, small one-room houses, hotels consisting of just a few huts or cottages near the beach. No sign of the high-rises that dominate today's Kuta.

We flew to Hong Kong to view the dragon boats in the harbour and the over-rated bargains, then on to fascinating Japan. Funds were rapidly diminishing but fortunately at that point we were heading homeward, as even in 1973 a cantaloupe in Tokyo cost ten dollars.

After months of unknown sanitation and uncertain drinking water, we could finally relax in Japan. I couldn't read the signs or be understood by anyone, but everything was sparkling clean. We spent three thrilling weeks touring the country—impossibly expensive to do now.

Hawaii definitely felt like 'coming home' in spite of the weird flowered muumuus the women wore and the strange American accent. Arriving in San Francisco, the first place I had visited before, I knew Toronto was not far off. Finally, in June 1973 we arrived back home. I was skinny and penniless but rich with memories.

In the preceding nine months, I had toured many foreign countries where I was in the minority and the world functioned normally for everyone else. I'd been forced to navigate the situation, whether it was 'WAWA', a purse-snatching, the *überkommandante*, or paranoia-inducing hash on a mountain top in Nepal. Constantly on the move, planning the next destination, I'd felt like a hobo, self-reliant, travelling with all I owned in my bag, an anonymous face in the crowd. Coming back to a land with people I knew, safe tap water and familiar food, I thought it would be easy to adjust, but it wasn't. The pressure was suddenly on to stay in one spot, set down roots and get established with a home and career in Toronto. So for me, the real culture shock was coming home.

Jon and I moved back into my mother's welcoming, comfortable, roomy home where we had stayed temporarily before we left. Suddenly I had a choice about what T-shirt, pants or shoes to wear. Life was complicated again. I had to force myself to call friends and look for work. I thought I could only handle something temporary rather than commit to a real practice of my own, like a grown-up. Locums would leave me with options in case I suddenly felt the need to take off again. But Jon seemed content to look for something more permanent.

Aside from my internship, my experience in medicine had not been particularly happy: all drudgery and hard work with few self-affirming incidents. Travel had opened my eyes and heart to the world. I saw grit and opulence, experienced hardship and beauty, learned about poverty and privilege. I hoped that my experiences abroad would better equip me to deal with the ongoing rigor of my career but the dread soon re-surfaced of having to face medical superiors in Toronto treating me like a punk again.

So it was not with great gusto that I set out for my first locum interview. Back to 'Scarberia', to the intersection of Danforth Road and Avenue, to a small brick house sitting beside a bus stop with industrial buildings on all sides. Walking up the front steps, I flashed on Dr Frank and his bottles. I didn't want a repeat of that uncertainty, fear and responsibility. If this didn't work out, I decided I'd simply take off and travel again. But I had no money.

Stepping into the shabby building with peeling yellowed walls, I was greeted by Bev, the receptionist, a friendly, middle-aged woman.

"This is an unusual practice," she began. "There are no appointments. The hours are posted on the door and all patients who arrive before closing time are seen. Some evenings, when we lock the door and leave at nine, the doctors are still here at 11 pm, seeing every last patient in the waiting room. And after they're done, they often make house calls, too."

After rave reviews by Bev and the nurse, who had both been there for almost twenty years, and because they were offering twenty per cent more than Frank had paid, I agreed to take the job.

I was surprised by the grunge of the place and the unusual pattern of practice. It sounded really old-fashioned, with a couple of old geezers from the dark ages. In Toronto, I was used to patients booking appointments for set time periods, like ten or fifteen minutes, so the schedule was fixed and only emergencies were added at the last minute. I thought it would be hard to work in such a foreign way—the irony being that I had just come from practising in Africa. Dr Frank's office was more typical-looking, newer, shinier, with fixed appointments, but it also functioned weirdly. Maybe all doctors were peculiar in their own way and it would be my journey to discover what would work for me?

The first weeks flew by. I rarely saw either doctor. Dr Szabo was on vacation. Jones and I shared one office, but were never there at the same time.

Three weeks later, I finally met Dr Szabo, who was a tall, polite gentleman with a distinguished east European accent. He reminded me of Dr Finestine in his absent-minded professorial way, yet was extremely attentive and treated everyone with great respect. Jones, short, skinny and Canadian, always left the rooms neat and tidy. When I worked opposite Dr Szabo, there was a trail of his every procedure left behind.

The patients were working-class from the area and were as devoted to the doctors as they were to their patients. I loved listening to admiring stories the patients told about both doctors. Another oddity in that office was that patient charts were filed by family, so the patients and I often had to sort through a lot of pages to find the appropriate ones. But they were invariably cooperative and it became a kind of game.

The work had a lovely pace—I took turns replacing one doctor for three weeks and then the other. I handled patients as I chose and both doctors were happy to help with any questions or problems I had. They never queried my decisions and there was never a hint of sexism. My self-esteem grew as I handled difficult problems with positive outcomes. I finally felt like an independent, practising physician.

I was learning more about flexibility and adaptability and once again how situations are not determined by the physical set-up of a place, but by the people running them. I was beginning to have an idea about how and where and with whom I'd like to practice—a downtown, working class area with 'real' people and 'real' problems, people who appreciated my help and didn't expect to be treated any better or worse than the next person. I didn't want a practice full of patients like some I'd run into in the ER—snooty, demanding and entitled.

I was stunned years later when I read in the College of Physicians and Surgeons Bulletin that charges had been laid against Dr Szabo for sexual impropriety. It seemed outrageous. Of all the doctors I had worked with, those two seemed the least likely to be guilty of anything like that. I regret that I didn't call to offer help as a character or professional witness but at the time I didn't think that was possible. I could only imagine how awful an ordeal it must have been for the doctor and the entire office staff until he was finally completely exonerated of all the charges.

When I recently read a notice of his death at the age of eighty-one, I wished I had told him how important working with him had been to me.

CHAPTER 8

Goldglass and Elvis

Late in 1973, Jonathan and I were invited to a 'salon' in a very fashionable Deer Park home on Walmsley Avenue in Toronto. The house was newly renovated with a beautiful old-fashioned fireplace in the sprawling front hall and many stained glass windows. We wandered around, observing well-dressed, sophisticated people in every room, finally finding the host and his wife in the sparkling pea-green Italian-style kitchen. Bob was an older colleague, a friend of a friend, a bright, hard-working guy with some pretty avant-garde ideas. Six-foot-two, with long, dark, straggly hair and dressed in a black, short-sleeved shirt, he greeted us with a bright smile.

Immediately offering us a glass of white wine, he introduced his wife, Dawn and then several of his guests: a lawyer, a businessman and a social worker. Loaded trays of hors d'oeuvres were passed around by uniformed waitresses.

An hour or so into the party, Bob called me aside to join him on my own in one of his many cosy little ante-rooms with fireplace. He was interested in finding a woman-doctor to work for him in his General Practice on Church Street, taking on his patients while he was pre-occupied with 'other pursuits' outside medicine.

He had an inner-city practice with lots of interesting pathology and planned to continue running the business end of the office, maintaining ownership of the lease and furniture. I could come in three days a week and earn sixty per cent of the fees billed. He would work the other two days with selective patients, people with whom he'd had a special relationship or had counselled. There was another doctor in the office but their practices were separate, except for emergency holiday coverage. I listened to him talk with one eye on the urbane crowd around us. "Call my secretary and set up a meeting with me," he said and dashed off to greet new arrivals.

Standing up to search for Jonathan, my head was spinning. More culture shock. I had been off travelling and doing locums while colleagues were moving forward in their lives. Bob had collected this very classy assortment of friends, restored an old home to its former splendour and started a practice from which he was already moving on.

Here we were, with no money, no new fancy friends, having finally left my mother's house for a rented apartment. I was not in competition with my colleagues but I certainly felt like an under-achiever, at least until I remembered my wealth of travel experience.

Jonathan and I had decided to set up separate offices because we wanted to work different areas of the city and I wanted to be independent in my work life. He had already established a practice in a middle class area uptown. Bob's proposition was an opportunity for me to work downtown where I wanted to be. I could take advantage of his efforts in establishing the practice and finally have my own long-term patients.

It struck me as weird that at an evening soirée I'd been offered a business proposal and how odd that he was telling me to book an appointment with him through his secretary. My experience was that colleagues arranged their own meetings with a clear separation of work from play. Nowadays such business dealings are routine but not so in 1973. Or was I still out of touch from my travels with life in the real world?

A week later, I climbed the front stairs of a sterile concrete building on Church Street. The first door on the right of a narrow, lifeless corridor bore his name, Dr Bob Goldglass and beneath it Dr Elvis Da Silva. I gingerly opened the door on a brightly-painted office with tasteful art along the walls, armchairs upholstered in a dark tweedy fabric and Berber carpet covering the floor.

The stench from cigarette smoke was overpowering. Two women were busy filling their ashtrays as they sat behind enormous wooden desks and dominated the large, open, waiting area. The older, stocky, grey-haired dame spit Irish-accented orders at the younger one, who busied herself telling patients where to sit and what to do.

I was directed to Bob's office, where he sat at a massive mahogany desk next to large windows overlooking Church Street. He greeted me briefly, asked for any questions about the practice and showed me into his separate examining room, with its shiny new beige examining table and cabinets. Then he led me across the packed waiting room where he introduced me to Dr Da Silva, a tall, dark-haired, charming man my age, with a warm handshake. After a brief chat, Bob showed me to the door and asked that I get back to him soon with a decision.

I was excited. I loved the area. The practice sounded interesting, varied and challenging, with many available specialists. I might actually have a regular income and could work as many or as few hours as I wished. I would finally be a grown-up doctor!

When opportunities arose for me in those days, I insisted upon rationally weighing the pros and cons, even though I could afford to gamble. In this case, the cigarettes were my biggest reservation. I had never smoked and hated the dull, cloying residue it left. At that time, smoking was still allowed indoors, even in doctors' offices. Although I could have stayed longer at Szabo and Jones, this project intrigued me and whatever the drawbacks, I succumbed to the excitement of something new.

I began working my three days a week and loved it. Over the first month, I saw young kids from Regent Park housing complex; old ladies from Ontario Housing apartments; professionals moving into the neighbourhood as it was being 'white-painted', or converted from rooming houses to fancy new renovated yuppie housing; and lots of gays who were just then establishing the community there.

My clothes reeked at the end of the day, but otherwise I was content. Frequently Elvis and I went for lunch to a local greasy spoon—a dingy, deep-fried-smelling place nearby. We ate Greek salad and rice pudding and traded personal stories from our past and medical problems from our present.

A couple of months later, I arrived at the office one morning to find bearded Chassidic men—from the ultra-Orthodox Jewish community at the other end of the city—sitting in the waiting room. I tried to imagine what sort of connection they had with Bob, an entirely secular, nonreligious person. They weren't booked as patients and when I asked Bob about them later, his response was mysterious. I was left curious about the Chassidim and Bob's 'other pursuits' outside of medicine and though I questioned him several times, I never got an explanation. I was intrigued, but never suspicious.

Three months into my work there, Elvis called me into his office and closed the door. He said he'd found irregularities in Bob's billings. On the days Bob was not in the office, he'd been billing and getting paid by the government for one-hour sessions of counselling with patients with 'No Phone' or 'No Fixed Address'.

"So you mean Bob's claiming for services he never provided to actual people who cannot be contacted for confirmation because they have no permanent address or phone number?"

"Exactly," he said.

I was astonished. I didn't know what to say. My first impulse was to quit the office in order to avoid trouble with the College of Physicians and Surgeons because of implication by association.

Elvis didn't agree. He had a well-established practice he enjoyed and he wasn't prepared to walk. He suggested we confront Bob with the evidence and give him the opportunity to explain. If he couldn't, then we would give him the option to either leave the practice so we wouldn't be implicated, or we would be forced to report his improper billings to the College.

I was upset. Bob had impressed me with his ease around business matters and I trusted his skills. I was suddenly witnessing another doctor falling off his pedestal—a recurring theme. What was it in medicine that attracted the Fist/Frank/Bob types? Or were there weirdos in every profession? Or was this just a long string of bad luck? Or did I embark on too many exciting propositions I should have avoided?

One week later, Elvis and I scheduled a meeting in the early evening after Bob's posse of staff had left with their cigarettes. We were both nervous. Elvis appeared in a black-leather jacket and steel-toed boots. Bob, in his usual cheery manner, walked in, sat down and asked what the meeting was about.

"We are uncomfortable," Elvis said. "We've discovered some irregularities in your billings."

"What do you mean?" Bob sounded shocked.

"You know what we're talking about," I declared. "Your billings for patients on days when you weren't in the office."

Silence.

Elvis continued: "We don't want to be implicated. Unless you quit working here and leave us in charge, we're going to report you."

Silence.

Elvis stood up, looming very close to Bob. "We'll give you twenty-four hours to get out."

Bob got up, headed for the door.

"Twenty-four hours," Elvis repeated as the door closed.

"I'll believe it when I see it," I mumbled. I didn't sleep at all that night.

The next morning, I trepidatiously climbed the long front staircase to discover Dr Goldglass's nameplate missing from the front door. Opening it, I was hit with stale smoke, but no fresh cigarettes burning and no one at the desks. The phones were ringing non-stop. Elvis was quietly seeing his patients as usual and mine were waiting. I buzzed Elvis on the intercom from my office and he came over when he was free.

"He's gone," he said. "Took all his appointment books and OHIP records and his secretaries and vanished." Elvis had asked our telephone answering service, Able Assistants, to take all calls until we could hire new staff and in the meantime we could ring them for messages. We had the locks changed, awaiting whatever repercussions from Bob.

Later that week, we hired Irene, a non-smoking receptionist, who knew medical billing inside out. Although we paid her half her former salary without the benefits of the Ministry of Health (where she'd worked previously), she simply wanted a job where her abilities would be appreciated. On her own, she accomplished more than what had formerly been done by two women. Her multitude of skills was matched by her capacious body and voluminous laugh. We were constantly entertained by her Scottish jokes as she effortlessly conducted patients in and out of the office.

I was aghast at what had gone on in that office in such a short time. I couldn't believe we had actually confronted Bob and he had said nothing. All of us had worked hard to obtain our medical degrees, taking the Hippocratic Oath in which we pledged to 'do no harm' to our patients.

His dishonesty was harming the universal medical care in Canada that we were so proud of and thereby harming a lot of patients by ripping off and depleting the system. But our plan had worked. Once again, speaking up to a more senior colleague had served me well. But how often was this pattern going to repeat itself? I thought medicine was about caring for patients. How many times would I find myself playing policewoman with my colleagues? The gilt continued to fall off the ideal doctor statue. At least I'd had one good experience with Szabo and Jones.

Some months later, Bob called me with a reasonable offer to buy his share of the furniture and transfer the lease into my name. I was totally suspicious of his intent, but it turned out to be a surprisingly smooth transaction. Someone who appeared so monstrous and unscrupulous in his actions had suddenly turned into a compliant puppy dog. So much so that I began to doubt his guilt. But such is the talent of some people: they suck you in with their charm, then cleverly feign guilt so you end up second-guessing yourself. They are left temporarily with an untarnished image… until all the evidence comes barrelling out at once.

Years later, when I was asked by another colleague to write a letter of support regarding her pattern of practice to the Medical Review Committee of the Ontario College of Physicians and Surgeons, where she was being charged with over-billing the system, I was reminded of the Bob situation. The irony being that this innocent woman, who treated patients in a holistic way, spending as much time as necessary with each one, was put through the horrors of accusation, defence lawyers and court proceedings with ultimate unfair re-payment of hundreds of thousands of dollars for services *actually* rendered. Yet it seems this man got away with billing for patients never seen. At the time I was young and inexperienced and didn't want to tarnish my name by association, but did we deal correctly with the situation by kicking him out and not reporting him to the College as well? Once again, I ended up doubting myself.

Elvis and I continued to work side by side for several years. My patients were intriguing—one was a fifteen-year-old girl whose baby was being cared for by her mother who was also a patient. I saw a woman who wanted her fingernails extracted so they would grow in more attractively. I spoke with a lawyer who only wanted to get pregnant if she could time the baby to be born precisely between the end of her Bar Ad exams and the beginning of her articling. I had to carefully explain to a young male patient about professional boundary issues because he couldn't understand why I wouldn't meet him in a coffee shop after hours to discuss his problems.

Elvis's patients were fascinating as well. He saw one woman who sat in the waiting room, rocking back and forth in her chair, singing to herself and smiling. One of his cheerful alcoholics would leave a puddle on the upholstered waiting room chair after every visit.

Over time, Elvis and I became good friends and would get together outside the office with our spouses. We went for rowdy dinners at a local haunt on Church Street where we knew the owner. We would start drinking and eating early and afterwards went back to one of our houses to continue carousing. Those were the wild party years of the '70s, before we all had kids.

One year, Elvis got itchy to do something new and turned his sights on politics. He had always been interested in social justice issues and was asked to run for provincial parliament as a member of the New Democratic Party in Rosedale. His mighty opponent was the elected representative for sixteen years from the then-powerful Progressive Conservative Party. He didn't have a great chance, or even a slim one, but we all had faith in him. He was the popular local GP, loved by all his patients, active on the community centre board and an emergency physician at St Michael's Hospital.

At the start of the campaign, I wrote a fundraising letter to all the area doctors, resulting in very generous donations from obvious and also from unexpected sources. Elvis appeared to be on his way. Overnight, campaign headquarters materialized downstairs in our office building—a crew of volunteers, desks, phones, bulletin boards, election signs and posters, all in orange and brown, the colours of the NDP at the time.

For weeks, Candidate Elvis gave resounding speeches at all-party meetings and I became his backroom political supporter. We brainstormed his talks, lunching at a slightly more upscale bistro at a table opposite the men in suits running the Big Blue Machine for his opponent. We discussed the issues of two-tiered health care, ex-psychiatric patient housing, day-care spots, neighbourhood green space and the privatization of hydro and gas utilities.

Towards the end of the race, before the office would open at 8 am, he and I stood outside the Yonge subway stations handing out pamphlets. I called potential NDP supporters, went door-to-door speaking to folks, stuffed envelopes and picked up the phones. I answered policy questions to which I didn't realize I knew the responses. I was busy continuously, either with patient care or with the campaign. The excitement built—lots of dances and parties, which were spirit-rousing and fund-raising.

Elvis did not miss a day in the office and I never had to see his patients for him. He did two jobs as if he'd always worked that way. Patients were excited that their doctor might also become their MPP. They volunteered to help out in any way they could. Our secretary took his campaign calls, relayed his messages and took deliveries. It was seamless, as if his election campaign had always been part of our office routine. For eight weeks, the campaign ran efficiently. Elvis was determined and it was hard not to get caught up in his enthusiasm.

On Election Day, I was an NDP scrutineer at Riverdale Hospital, my job to ensure that nothing unusual was going on at the poll. Hospital patients came and went in their wheelchairs. Outside people wandered in, bewildered, proud to be there, pleased with themselves that they were voting. It was a long, intense day. At 8 pm the polls closed, the tension mounted, and I headed over to the local church basement.

Elvis was pumped. The numbers started to come in. They were mostly for his opponent, but a good sum for him. The music pounded as the Big Blue Machine rolled over him. It was all done quickly, but we had a fun party afterward.

The next day, we returned to our medical practice, which functioned at half-steam. We'd gotten used to double-duty and walked around looking for extra work to do. Once again, the practice of medicine had taken me into arenas I'd never dreamed I would explore.

Many years later, I spoke to a friend who had worked tirelessly with her doctor-husband on the campaign. Because Elvis was a friend of mine, they had never revealed to me their feelings of being exploited, then discarded, so they subsequently distanced themselves from him. They saw another snake in the office long before I did.

CHAPTER 9

General Practice: From Seniors to Babies and Everyone in Between

In the '70s, the excitement of general practice never waned. The office was always busy with phone calls, drop-ins, sick children, prescription renewals and hospital visits. My days on Church Street were lively and peripatetic. Often, Murphy's Law kicked in—whatever can go wrong, will go wrong.

One Friday afternoon, as I was working my way through people with pussy red throats, yellow vaginal discharges and pink rashy cheeks, my receptionist Irene brought me a note: 'Mrs Justen, 295 Shuter Street. Seen by Nurse. Fever, short of breath. Looks really sick. Needs house call.'

I knew Mrs Justen would never let the nurse phone unless it was serious.

My long day was not about to end without a trip into the community to see one of my favourite patients, a spry, full-of-fun, ninety-three-year-old. Because of arthritis in her back and knees, Mrs Justen could get around her own apartment with a walker, but she rarely got further than the hallways of her building, so I saw her every two months for routine care in her home. She had a 'visiting homemaker' bring her groceries and the Victorian Order of Nurses went in regularly to check her blood pressure and make sure she was taking her anti-inflammatory medications.

General Practice was different then. Teams of community family doctors and public health nurses looked after the elderly in their homes. If necessary, the team had the back-up of hospitals where these people could be admitted for a few days for an acute illness like pneumonia or dehydration and then return home in better shape for ongoing care by people they knew and trusted. This system in Ontario seemed to vanish for many years in the '80s and '90s, when old folks were routinely institutionalized. Only recently has there been a shift back to this goal of keeping people in their own homes for as long as possible via community help.

Although we were once taught to address our patients with 'Mr Mrs or Miss', in my office, in order to maintain a non-threatening atmosphere, I usually preferred to call people by their first names. Except with Mrs Justen. She had asked me several times to call her Anne, but I couldn't bring myself to do so with such a formal, classy woman, who, in retirement, was forced to live in subsidized housing.

After the waiting room had emptied, I grabbed my trusty brown leather doctor's bag (purchased on a trip to Italy, circa 1973), hopped into my car and revved down Church Street to Shuter, turning eastward to the grotty Moss Park high-rise complex. I got out of my car, walked past residents lined up in their lawn chairs on either side of the front door. Knowing I was there to see Mrs Justen, they gave me a quick report on her worsening condition.

I waited fifteen minutes for the sighing old elevator to carry me upwards, clunking to a stop on the eighth floor. The doors opened with reluctant creakiness and I stepped out onto red plaid carpet.

Mrs Justen's door, marked with a fresh-smelling lavender wreath, was slightly ajar. I found her sitting on the edge of a pink brocade couch, leaning forward between coughs, every breath an effort. She offered to make me a cup of tea, but I encouraged her to sit still to conserve her precious energy. I proceeded to examine her and concluded that she had pneumonia, and as she lived alone, she would need to be cared for in hospital.

After informing her seventy-year-old daughter what was happening and calling an ambulance, I scurried down the eight flights of stairs, avoiding the molasses elevator to head off to my evening dinner-party.

After greeting my hosts, I used their phone to inform the hospital of Mrs Justen's impending arrival. The first-year resident on-call for internal medicine, rudely retorted:

"Why are you calling *me*? First she needs to be assessed by the emergency doctor and if he refers her to me, only then will she be admitted if I deem it necessary."

Without bothering to convince him, I asked to speak to his superior. His calm response was that Dr Moons, his boss, would be angry if I bothered him on a Friday evening. I nevertheless contacted Moons and explaining what had gone on with Mrs Justen, found myself lecturing:

"It's a waste of precious health care dollars to pay me to make a house call and diagnosis and then have the emergency physician assess the patient all over again. Why employ experienced physicians in the community if young residents in hospital think they know better? *We* are the ones who are familiar with our patients, and for me, she is *not* just another ninety-three-year-old to be disposed of in emerg."

It worked. Dr Moons listened carefully and called back later to say Mrs Justen had been admitted to his service. Mrs Justen recovered well from her pneumonia, and one week later I visited her again in her apartment and put her back on my regular roster for maintenance house calls every two months.

I was determined not to be caught in a tug-of-war with the resident, refusing to be demeaned and undermined by this recently graduated student who was looking out for himself and trying to lighten his workload by seeing as few people as possible. He felt entitled to behave that way, possibly because I was a woman, but likely because I was not on staff at the hospital. The hierarchy in the 'Ivory Tower' of the teaching hospital had followed me out into my practice.

Once again, as intimidating as it was for me to contradict another physician, I spoke up for myself. Not an atypical experience. Dr Samuel Shem's book, *House of God*, details the goings-on in American teaching hospitals in the '70s, where resident doctors often referred to old people as 'Gomers'— 'Get Out of My Emergency Room'. The goal in emerg was to 'Buff and Turf' that is, either quickly make the elderly seem well enough to go home, or get rid of them to another department just to get them out.

Even today old people are never regarded as being interesting or 'sexy cases' because they have chronic illnesses. Rarely do they have dramatic diagnoses, which, when uncovered, are considered a 'coup'—the specialty of television heroes like Dr House who constantly appear brilliant.

Over the years, I worked hard to improve communication between doctors inside and out of hospital. With the help of a cardiologist, who recognized the contribution of GPs out there 'in the trenches', we made an attempt to get copies of treatment notes from the emergency department mailed to family doctors who would see the patients for follow-up. Unfortunately, as soon as complaints about the clerical load surfaced, the plan was discontinued and GPs were shipped back into oblivion.

Almost thirty years later 'Dr Shem' wrote a sequel, *Mount Misery*, about an elite psychiatric hospital's fierce competition between physicians and low regard for patients. So it seems that little has changed and I'm certain such blatant hegemony contributed to my growing feeling of distance from the hospital milieu.

One bustling Friday afternoon I took a call from a criminal lawyer (also a patient) asking for a favour. He had a client he thought was not getting very good medical care in the Don Jail, nearby and needed an outside physician to visit immediately. Up on charges of attempted murder with a court appearance the following Monday, the man was unable to sleep and wanted Valium but the jail doctor refused. I agreed to see him.

After finishing at the office, I raced up to my mother's house at Bathurst and Eglinton to gulp down some of her yummy cornflake chicken, but was too edgy to enjoy her luscious chocolate cake with icing. I wasn't keen on making the long drive back downtown alone, especially to the Don Jail, so I asked Lynni, my fifteen-year-old sister, to join me. Having nothing much else going on, she agreed. My mother was not pleased to let Lynni go but she also wasn't keen to see me go alone, so off we went.

Overlooking the Don Valley at Gerrard, the Don Jail is a Renaissance Revival-style grand dame built in 1864, with a circular drive at the entrance. Craning our necks to check out the building overhead, we walked up to the brooding blackened stone structure and pushed open the enormous ancient wooden doors leading into a rotunda, where we were met by a security guard.

Lynni was abruptly told to wait in the front entrance hall under the enormous cupola while I was led off through the dark, dank halls. A brusque nurse ushered me into a small room with twenty-foot ceilings, which was totally empty except for an old examining table and two wooden chairs. She motioned for me to sit in one, she sat in the other. The patient arrived in handcuffs with a second guard and was told to sit on the examining table.

A big guy with dishevelled short hair and fresh stubble on his cheeks said he needed sleep.

"I'd like to ask you a few questions first."

"Shoot."

"How long have you had trouble sleeping?"

"Forever," he replied.

"Have you ever taken medication for it?" I suspected I was hitting a minefield, but I proceeded.

"I take all kinds of uppers and downers all the time... out there," he answered.

"Are you on any other pills right now?" I tried to stay the course. "Have you ever been diagnosed with a mood disorder?"

"No... whatever the hell that is. Look, I never answer questions when I score Valium on the street. That's what I need right now."

"Do you have any other illnesses or allergies?" I continued.

"I'm allergic to nosey doctors asking a whole lot of useless questions!"

I completed the routine inquiries. I felt like I was on centre-stage in front of the nurse and the guard, who were clearly a lot more experienced in this situation. I mentally scrolled through the medico-legal requirements in order to write a prescription, and with anxiety rising and the stuffy air beginning to cloud my brain, soon succumbed to giving him what he wanted in order to get out of there. I wrote a prescription for 30 Valium 5mgm, and handed it to the nurse, who rolled her eyes and nodded. Walking towards the door, I muttered to the inmate: "Good luck."

Bounding down the darkened hall, I found Lynni sitting on the window ledge, with her feet tucked under her.

"Am I glad to see you!" she said. "I was terrified. I had to sit on my feet to keep them out of the way of the rats and mice running back and forth across the floor." I mumbled an apology and we quickly headed out into the stifling evening August air, which at that moment felt strangely fresh.

All my optimism about sincerely caring for people in an egalitarian way was slowly being crushed. Innocently enough, I had dragged myself and my teenage sister into what I thought would be a helping situation. I figured that if a lawyer could deal with this kind of client, so could I. Only later did I understand that in order to build rapport, he probably saw the man on multiple occasions and under very different circumstances. Once again I realized how much I still had to learn and how I was the only one who could take care of myself. And looking out for me, I would have to face flack from others, be they doctors, lawyers, patients, or even family members. My self-protective skills would constantly need to be honed, in the same way that Lynni quickly learned to protect herself from the rodents under the rotunda.

Throughout the haze of office days in general practice, each patient's narrative enveloped me in work that I loved. I often forgot about items simmering on the back burner all day, which usually came to a boil as the waiting room cleared.

One day, I received a call from Teddy Frenckel, a high school buddy who had become a GP in Barrie. I was thrilled to hear from him. We hadn't spoken since our days together at Vaughan Road Collegiate at least twenty years before. He explained that some years earlier he had received a letter from another colleague of ours, Jessie. She and her husband David wanted to adopt a newborn. When Ted discovered a teenager in his practice who definitely decided to give up her baby, he immediately called Jessie. She informed him that they already had a little boy, but suggested Ted call me, because Jessie knew my cousin was looking for a baby. He was informing me of the imminent birth. I was delighted. I took down the details: the baby was due in three months, had healthy parents aged eighteen and nineteen and the mother was certain about the adoption because she had already enrolled in university in the fall. I promised to call my cousin Sandi at the end of the day and get back to him.

Although I was 'child-free', as we called it then, the thought of an infant going to a happy home where he or she was totally yearned for filled my heart with pleasure. This one day I was able to skip happily through my patients, never forgetting the joyous task I was facing at the end of the day, a call to my cousin Sandi to give her the wonderful news.

Back in the '70s, unplanned pregnancy was a huge issue. There was not yet widespread access to the birth control pill. Therapeutic abortions were only performed in limited numbers at few hospitals and had to be approved by a committee and include letters of recommendation by two doctors. Social factors, such as the mother's economic situation, her age and her educational status were not considered adequate reasons to recommend abortion. The only other safe place was the Morgentaler Clinic which was repeatedly shut down because therapeutic abortion was not yet legal in Ontario, so the services were sporadic and cloaked with stigma.

Some desperate women crossed the border into the US for the procedure at huge expense. Others were forced into 'backroom' methods, which often led to catastrophes. The net result was many unplanned pregnancies going to term, often in teenage girls who were sent away to the big city to 'homes for unwed mothers' by parents so ashamed of their daughter's pregnancy, they made the decision for adoption without consent of either biological parent.

After enduring months in the homes, often cared for by unsympathetic or religious older staff, the girls were never given the opportunity to see the baby before being shipped back to their communities and expected to carry on as if nothing had happened. The 'shame' had 'gone away', but the mother's enormous experience of loss was never addressed.

On the other hand, there were few, if any, fertility clinics so it was common practice for couples unable to conceive to try to adopt one of these babies by writing letters across the province to doctors who might have a patient willing to 'give up' their child.

I received one or two such letters per month, intimately detailing a couple's situation and their desperation to become parents of a newborn—such adoptions were mostly private. Older children were usually placed by the Children's Aid Society, kids from families with what were then euphemistically called 'social' problems, wherein the issue of maternal use of drugs or alcohol was never openly discussed.

With the waiting room finally empty, rummaging through bits of paper on my desk for Sandi's number, I sat down at my antique roll-top. My hands were shaking. I got up, dumped out my stale cup of coffee, refilled it with tap water, sat down again, then dialled the number.

"Sandi, how are you? It's Sharon Baltman," I said, my voice cracking with emotion. "I'm calling to say I've found a baby for you."

"Oh my God Sharon, I was just about to call you. We have a baby. A little boy. He's coming home with us in two weeks," she practically cried into the phone. "It's raining babies."

"That's wonderful. I'm very happy for you."

"We'll invite you to the *bris*. Thank you so much for calling."

I wished her luck with her little guy and hanging up the phone, stared at it, dumbfounded. I didn't know what to do next. I felt as if I was on a roller coaster. I was thrilled for Sandi, but what about this poor baby? I called Teddy and told him what happened and he reassured me that we'd find another home.

Then I remembered: "Actually, the other doctor in my office said he had a patient who's wanted to adopt for ages. She'd almost given up because she only wanted a newborn. I'm sure she'd be ecstatic. I'll speak to him and call you back. I'm beginning to feel like a baby trader."

Elvis confirmed his patient was still interested, but I asked him to hold off until I had spoken to Jessie. She had directed Ted to me about this baby and I wanted to be open and fair to everyone involved in such a serious and delicate matter.

I called Jessie and told her about my cousin and that we were planning to notify Elvis's patient about the baby.

"You can't do that!" Jessie exclaimed.

"Excuse me?" I gulped.

"That's *our* baby. We sent out letters," Jessie insisted angrily.

"But you already adopted a baby," I reasoned.

"No. We sent Ted to you when he called us about this baby. He only called you because I told him to. You said you wanted a baby for your cousin. If your cousin already has a baby, then this baby is *ours* to pass along, not *yours*," Jessie stated.

"I don't understand," I attempted. "What does it matter who does the referral, as long as the baby gets a good home?"

"My husband David already promised the next baby we heard about to another woman, so this one belongs to her. You no longer have to be involved. I'll look after it with Ted," and she hung up on me.

It seemed that David fancied himself as some kind of baby conduit, the godfather of newborns. He dispensed them to would-be moms and dads on his list, according to some priorities he established—nurses, downtown doctors and friends of doctors. I had never thought there could be such competition between people, let alone colleagues. It wasn't until September 2011, that I learned from a CBC radio documentary about the huge significance in those private adoptions of cold, hard cash.

CHAPTER 10

Never a Dull Moment

No longer travelling to far-off lands or doing itinerant locums and now established in our respective practices, Jonathan and I decided to do what was *de rigueur* for young married couples at the time—buy a house. We eventually found a pink stone, three-storey on Lawton Boulevard near Yonge and St Clair for what seemed like a high price: $120,000. Being optimistic and a bit naive, we didn't realize how much work an old house required, but we soon turned it into a warm, welcoming abode.

A cute, nattily-dressed young doctor had recently joined Jonathan in his busy general practice. One day, Charles stopped by the house for a drink after work. Then he dropped by the next night and the night after that. He was warm and friendly, brought flowers, wine, dope and cassette tapes of the Pointer Sisters and Ike and Tina Turner. He cooked chilli dinners and we partied late into the night in front of the raging fireplace. We talked about medicine, our patients, our colleagues. Like many GPs, Charles worked in the emergency department as well as in private practice. He told me about his 'brilliant diagnosis' in emerg of an abdominal aneurysm in a man whose only symptom was vomiting. He picked up an inflamed appendix in a little boy. He was very proud of his clinical abilities.

I became concerned when he drove, half-stoned, straight from my place to his emergency shift at the hospital. I worried about the people he was treating. I got angry with him, but had no idea what to do. I wanted to confront him, but I didn't have the confidence to do so without Jonathan's approval. The partying continued. Eventually I summoned the courage to speak to Charles, who reassured me that in the car on his way to work, he always reviewed protocols for what he would do in any given situation. That worried me even more.

Then something changed about Charles's expressions and mannerisms. He started to walk like Jonathan, talk like him. It was totally creepy.

One Saturday, a few weeks later, Charles casually walked into my kitchen from the back door. The lights went off. He walked back out the door and they came on again. I immediately asked him to leave so Jonathan and I could figure out what was happening. The light-bulb had finally gone on for me and I realized that I had to get Charles out of my life. I told Jon how upset I was about Charles practising whilst stoned and I insisted that he tell Charles not to show up at the house anymore.

Charles continued to work in Jonathan's office for several more months. Then one day, he vanished. He simply did not show up for work and Jonathan had to see all his patients. He was never heard from again, although he apparently continued to practise medicine in a different area of Toronto. I didn't understand what happened then, nor do I understand it now.

The explanation for the kitchen incident with Charles was a loose wire under the floor, but it serendipitously provided me with an opportunity to deal with yet another doctor's troubling behaviour that I felt helpless to fix. Reporting him to the college was not done then.

In med school I had always thought I would stay up nights worrying about my own patients because I knew I would make mistakes—we are all human. In reality, I ended up worrying more about other doctors' patients when I was aware of some wrongdoing by the practitioner and remaining silent was difficult. A law has since been passed requiring doctors to report colleagues whenever we receive disturbing information about them from a patient. However, if a patient is not the source, the taboo on reporting may still exist.

Back then there were taboos of many sorts, another of them being that doctors did not practise anything but traditional Western medicine. I didn't understand why we couldn't incorporate other teachings into our work.

One day Elvis approached me about a weekend course offered by Dr Pindar, an Indian physician, teaching acupuncture skills to medical doctors. Along with several of my colleagues, I jumped at the opportunity to learn something new.

Dr Pindar had completed his Western medicine training, then followed a renowned healer all across China studying his Eastern techniques of acupuncture. He later became a highly-regarded teacher at a university in Bombay, and then an early pioneer spreading the study of acupuncture around the globe. He was a member of Cabinet in India's government, as well as a friend of top ministers. He was also reputed to be quite the ladies' man, using his sarong to hide his lascivious thoughts and responses.

Early one freezing Saturday morning in January of 1976 I raced into an old building on Wellesley Street, looking for room number 210 that turned out to be an over-heated, musty classroom on the second floor with a few beaten-up wooden chairs scattered about. I threw off my coat and desperately pushed open a heavy double-hung window to let in some fresh air. Just then, I heard the chatter of South Asian voices and the door behind me opened for the arrival of a handsome, stocky, brown-skinned man, surrounded by three men and a woman, all clad in sarongs over jeans.

"Good morning, I am Dr Pindar. Good to meet you," he said, and with a flourish, introduced his entourage and instructed them how to arrange the chairs and blackboard. They searched for the most comfortable spot for him. Then three of my colleagues stumbled in, apologizing for being late.

"Welcome to acupuncture," Pindar began, pointing to illustrations delineating the meridians or pathways in the body along which the energy or *qi* (pronounced 'chee') flows. Acupuncture points were clearly marked along the meridians. "We will begin with the basics. First, we find *Hegu*: the point between the thumb and first finger at the top of the fleshy bulge. It is the place we insert a needle for pain, any pain. Who would like to be the test subject for the first needle?"

Since I had a raging headache, I was eager to volunteer.

"Upon insertion, the needle creates a hot feeling," he explained, plunging the needle into my hand. "There is a slight throbbing, swelling and tingling. Then I take the needle and twiddle it. Sometimes I thrust it. And sometimes twiddling and thrusting. How is that, Dr Baltman?"

"It's okay, but my head still hurts," I answered, feeling the temperature in the room rising.

"That is not a problem. We will add another needle to *Bahui*. That is the point at the top of the head, where the line joining the ears intersects with a line up from the nose. It is the relaxation point. We use it a lot. It means 'penetrating heaven'. You will soon be relaxed and pain-free. It is all in the *qi*. Do not let it get dammed up. If the *qi* is dammed up, you must un-dam it!"

He continued to lecture about the correct angle of insertion, the specifics of placement for maximum effect and the medical ailments that could be cured.

"And never make acupuncture treatments easily available to people. Patients must chase you up a tree. Only then are they motivated and it will work for them."

"What about sterilization of the needles?" one of my colleagues asked innocently.

"Needles are too thin for bacteria to walk on," he replied. "And did you know that Toronto has the world's largest acupuncture needle? It is the CN tower. And besides, it's not about the needle with the prick, it's about the prick with the needle." He roared with laughter at his own jokes and talked non-stop all day.

Finally at 5 pm, he announced: "There is so much to teach you. We will stop now for the day, but resume tomorrow. Why don't you come to India for more intense study? I would like to invite all of you to dinner tonight. To my brother's house for a traditional Indian meal. Please, all of you, come. Samir will leave you a map," he stated and swept out the door with his harem, leaving us to figure out how to get to the town of Guelph, seventy kilometres from Toronto, by 8 pm.

My head exploding, I was exhausted. I raced out of the scorching room into the freezing cold to search for my car. The headache had started before Dr Pindar had put that first needle in *Hegu* and continued to worsen as the blaring old radiators increased the temperature in the room. I was entertained by his ditties—although he did hang on to my hand for an awfully long time—and fascinated by the subject matter, but I couldn't absorb much through my aching head.

I had hoped that acupuncture would be a new tool to add to my armamentarium for chronic pain in people who weren't responding to traditional Western treatments, but its lack of success with my own symptom was not exactly a reassuring testimonial. The weekend was costing me $300, a lot of money at the time, but I thought it would be exciting to study with him.

Acupuncture was exotic, a bit shady-sounding and definitely not paid for by OHIP (government healthcare). Relatives and friends thought I was crazy to embark on the study of such a 'radical' subject, yet the fact that it was not main-stream was exactly what attracted me.

I couldn't resist the offer of a social evening with this interesting group of people, which might take me back to our days of travel in India. I rested for a bit at home, got some relief from my aching head with several 222s, then joined the group heading out.

Towards 8 pm, after an hour-long car-ride, we found the bungalow in Guelph. We were warmly greeted and instantly surrounded by wall-to-wall people, all in saris and eastern pants. The sweet smell of masala and the swirly sounds of sitar music reminded me of my days in Udaipur and Jaipur. The bowl of green curry with rice and chicken tickled my palate.

I was mesmerized by the mixing of work and play. We had studied hard all day with this man and now he was feeding and entertaining us. He told silly jokes and insisted we join him with wine. The twinkle never left his eye as he kept coming up to us and introducing us as his loyal students. He loved having a group of Canadian doctors following him around, just as he'd tagged along behind his Chinese healer.

The next day, we endured another stretch of eight long hours in the sweltering room, but I learned a lot. I also laughed at his anecdotes and came to understand the theory of *qi*. I could remember names and locations of important acupuncture points along the meridians. It all seemed to make sense and I started to wonder why we never studied this in medical school, especially since there were so few adverse effects. Pindar wondered as well. He happily sold me some of the special needles, which I stored in solution in sterile plastic containers originally intended for urine cultures. *Voilà*, I was ready to practise acupuncture.

I began by inserting needles into myself, then into consenting colleagues, finally into friends and family members who agreed to be my guinea pigs. Most found relief from any current ache or pain. They felt the tingling, warmth and throbbing, exactly as described by Pindar. I soon felt confident and as there was no regulation of acupuncture practitioners at the time, began using my skills in the office to treat patients with unresponsive chronic pain, often achieving very good results.

I explained acupuncture to them, carefully avoiding some of Pindar's crude descriptions. Patients were soon willing to pay out-of-pocket because of their great relief and I was thrilled to have a new side-effect-free tool in my arsenal. I even tried, as Pindar had suggested, using my fingernail to do acupressure on a point on the midline above my upper lip as stimulation to keep myself awake when dozing off.

It was one of the few times in my learning career that teachers mixed socializing with medicine, so I was able to enjoy this man's wonky sense of humour and fun-loving attitude. And I also admired him for having created a beautiful amalgam of East and West via the mighty acupuncture needle.

Although acupuncture had been practiced for centuries in the East, in the 1970s it was practically unheard of in the West and resisted by those traditional practitioners who had heard of it. By the '90s it had become widespread and tightly regulated especially in urban centres. Many doctors now practise a combination of Western and Complementary Therapies including meditation, Traditional Chinese Medicine which includes acupuncture, as well as other non-Western modalities.

Back then, being at the forefront was very exciting. I was sad to give up acupuncture when I later left general practice in 1986 and will always be grateful to this outrageous man from India who had taught us, entertained us and imparted ancient wisdom in such a clear, memorable way.

PART II
FACE À FACE WITH LIFE

CHAPTER 11

In and Out of the Office

Aside from a few hiccoughs along the way, up to the age of 30 I had lived a charmed personal life. I grew up jokingly bemoaning the fact that I was the 'unloved middle child', yet everyone adored me. I'd never experienced death, except for my paternal grandmother, who died at 105. I was accepted into medical school, married the classmate I fell in love with and together we'd created a wonderful life, professional difficulties notwithstanding. Being of the 'Me Generation' of Baby Boomers, focused intently on developing ourselves, Jon and I were happy to travel and not be burdened by the worries of childcare—trips to Guatemala, France, and each summer, party cottages on Lake Simcoe.

Then suddenly, everything changed.

It was a Friday in June, 1977. I got a call from Jonathan to come home as soon as possible because he was having abdominal pain and feared it was appendicitis. I cancelled my patients and raced home to find him crying. My dermatologist had called to say the biopsy of the skin lesion removed from my thigh revealed a malignant melanoma. Jonathan wasn't sure, but he thought I needed more surgery.

"Why did she call *you*?" I asked, trying to search for her number. "What else did she say?" Attempting to get more details, I only elicited more tears.

When I finally spoke to Dr Joe, she described the situation to me, without explaining why I hadn't been the first to know. To treat the cancerous mole, she recommended a wider excision of the surrounding area, entailing plastic surgery with a skin graft to cover it and removal of the inguinal lymph nodes to see if the cancer had spread. She had arranged a bed for me at Sunnybrook the following Monday, where I would meet the plastic surgeon, but she had no idea how long I'd be in hospital.

As soon as I hung up the phone, I started to doubt the diagnosis. I wondered how I could just passively accept this elaborate plan. I was pissed off that she hadn't notified me first. It was the '70s and feminism was starting to take hold. I intentionally went to a woman doctor to be treated equally. Instead, Jonathan had been put in charge.

Then I thought that maybe there was a lab error. Perhaps I needed a second opinion? But no, that is what every family member and the entire Jewish community would do—ask questions, opt for another opinion, see the 'Best' doctor in town, go to Mount Sinai Hospital.

I decided I didn't want to do what everyone else would do. Although angry with her, I trusted Dr Joe and didn't want to complicate my life by running around the city chasing other opinions. I would do it my way: I would believe my physician and follow her advice. I would proceed as she had suggested. That would be my rebellion.

I was still in shock, but calmly went into auto-pilot mode. I had to get myself organized and available to go into hospital in three days. I had to cancel my patients and find another doctor to look after them. I had to notify my family and friends and decide what details to reveal to whom. I had to tidy up chores and bills at home and pack, having no idea what would be required for an indefinite hospital stay.

Dr Joe was clearly focused on getting me treated as quickly as possible, so I had no time to react emotionally. Jonathan was doing that for me.

In the '70s, cancer or 'The Big C' also known as the 'Real McCoy', was not dealt with openly and only spoken about in hushed tones. There were no fund-raising bike rides, no TV discussion programs, no 'Runs for the Cure'. I was a very private person and didn't want to answer questions from patients about my personal health. I didn't want to be seen as the victim, 'the doctor who had cancer'. So I decided not to tell my patients why I would be off work.

Then there was the issue of my perfectionist father who had just had a stroke and was dealing with an imperfect gait and inability to drive a car. Knowing his vulnerable state, I refused to inflict more worries upon him, especially if the plastic repair turned out less than ideal. Also my father-in-law was phobic about cancer—as Jonathan's mother had died of a colon malignancy when he was only fifteen. Her death had always been a taboo subject in their home. As a result, my decision to keep it all a big secret, except from my mother, my siblings and my close friends was the start of a whole series of secrets.

My mother came over to our house to hear my news in person. Through her tears, she revealed her dread of the month of June, because of her recurrent misfortunes in that month, the details of which she didn't reveal. Having deep faith in the Jewish religion, she promised to pray for me.

Monday morning arrived and I was admitted to hospital, luckily getting a private room. The stark sterility of the hospital space was soon broken by bursts of summer colour. My good friend Marilyn arrived in her orange and green florals with a bottle of deep red Dubonnet to toast *l'chaim* (to life). Friend Ruthie came crisp and gorgeous in her elegant white cotton suit. My younger brother Lawrie appeared in his grotty shorts and sweaty yellow T-shirt. My sister Lynni showed up in her coral knits with new white shoes. My mother brought one of her special dark chocolate cakes with icing, 'for when I felt like a piece'.

They all tried to appear cheerful and bright. The nurses poked their noses in periodically and wondered if there was a party going on.

Reduced to wearing a blue hospital gown, I sat looking as healthy and bright-eyed and normal as anyone, feeling well although I'd been told I was sick. Suddenly I was no longer the doctor in charge, giving orders. I felt helpless and lost in the mammoth hospital system.

I was worried, but convinced the only thing I could do was focus my energy on getting through the surgery and healing. I'd used acupuncture, biofeedback and hypnotic techniques to deal with my migraine headaches so I planned to use hypnosis again to muster my strength to help repair my body.

It was the early days of the Mind-Body work of Dr Carl Simonton in California, where he conducted studies on cancer patients using visualization techniques, which resulted in improved quality of life as well as increased survival times. I knew of his work through word-of-mouth, journal articles and books. Many were sceptical, but I was determined to try.

Before the surgery, I repeatedly relaxed into a trance of self-hypnosis, visualizing my body producing white horses galloping through my bloodstream eating up stray cancer cells. I found an accommodating anaesthetist to work with me and we agreed I would relax myself pre-operatively without calming drugs, and then in the operating room he would touch my shoulder to signal me to start breathing more deeply, so he could put me under with the usual pharmaceuticals. Later, I would imagine my skin graft sticking to my leg and healing over smoothly and softly and the donor site healing up quickly and thoroughly.

When it was time for surgery, two charming, usually very calm young men, Jonathan and Elvis, both green with worry, wheeled me down the hall. I felt like a goddess being fed bunches of round red seedless grapes, nurturing me back to health. My trance began.

After that, I remember little, except that hospital room again, filled with loving friends and relatives. There I was, stuck in a hospital bed. A big bulky dressing over my right lower thigh where they had excised a three by four inch area of tissue around the original lesion. I couldn't bend my right hip at the groin because of a second dressing where the lymph nodes had been removed and my skin stitched up. The side of my hip had a third bandage where the skin had been harvested to cover the defect created by the excision. I had to eat lying on my left side in order to keep my leg straight, although I was not keen to eat much of the hospital meals which looked and tasted like dog food. Everyone began bringing me delectable treats.

Healing was a slow process, even with my visualization techniques. In those days, they didn't quickly mobilize people after surgery, so by the time I did get onto my feet, I was constantly light-headed. I used mental images picturing the blood flowing to my head and circulating in my brain to maintain oxygen supply to keep me upright.

It was hard work. Bills and household chores and office details vanished. I forgot about patients and their concerns. My world had narrowed down to tunnel vision, eliminating the periphery. My entire focus was on basic bodily function and needs and healing.

The skin graft didn't take as quickly as expected. I was crushed. I had been hoping to go home after ten days, but had to stay for two weeks until it finally healed. The image of the flight of stairs at home felt like an Everest of a challenge. The thought of going back to being a doctor, looking after patients again, was daunting. I wondered how I could spend my time worrying about them when I didn't know how much time I had myself.

Maybe I needed to give up my practice and just focus on me? But I had spent so many years of hard work learning to do what I loved. So many confusing thoughts and so much time to think them. But whenever I felt down, there was always someone there to talk me through it with love and understanding. Every time I approached the underworld, someone threw me a raft.

Finally getting home, attempting to climb my several flights of steps was definitely challenging but I eventually managed. Then I had to deal with the ramifications of my diagnosis. The reality was that at age thirty, I had a malignant melanoma, a term I had often confused with multiple myeloma. They sounded similar, but what I had was a single malignant skin tumour. The lymph node resection confirmed that there was no cancer in them, but in order to be sure there were no lesions elsewhere, the doctors wanted to do a scan of my liver and spleen, as well as a bone scan. I did the former, but not wanting a lot of radiation to make me sicker and convinced that I was fine, I refused the bone scan.

My thoughts and fears glommed on to my mortality. Will I live to see 40, or even 35? What about kids? I'd never wanted children. I was too young and had other things to do—travel, career, friends. But suddenly I didn't want my life to be over without experiencing the immense life-affirming act of motherhood.

Because the melanoma had appeared shortly after I started taking birth control pills for the first time in my life, they suspected a causal relationship which had been reported in the literature. Therefore hormones or pregnancy were to be avoided for at least four to five years. When the rebel in me heard that I couldn't have something, it became all the more desirable. I also had to avoid the sun at all times forever, as it is still believed that excessive exposure to sun can lead to mutations in melanin cells in the skin, leading to melanomas years later. So all the sunburns I got as a teenager in the '60s on the pale delicate skin of my nose, shoulders and legs, which later peeled, could have caused my current condition. Who would have thought that those delicious warming beams could be so dangerous later on? Suddenly I had gone from a free-living doctor having fun to facing my fate.

In July, Jonathan and I went up to the cottage on Lake Simcoe as planned. I lay there on my bed, wondering what the hell would happen next. I visited with friends, I cried, we talked, we laughed, we wept. They brought me healthy home-cooked meals. And as the days passed, I became more mobile and started to feel well. To protect myself from the rays in which I had formerly loved to bask, I bought outrageous hats, dressed up in colourful full-length muumuus and slathered on gallons of sunscreen. There are photos of me covered entirely from head to toe, lying in the sun or water-skiing. This became part of my new persona.

One day at a time, I managed to carry on. I returned to work, keeping my secret about my absence close to my heart. It was hard going back. Again I wondered if I could take on the task of sorting through patients' ailments. My experience with cancer and being the patient had changed me. I now knew what it was like to be at the other end of doctor's orders. To be shuffled around and not heard by the medical staff. To deal with ramifications of a diagnosis. I also thought about what was important to me in life in the bigger picture. I wondered if this would make me more empathic or less. Slowly, my concern for patients returned and feeling strong, I remained optimistic. I went for check-ups after three months, then six months with the internist, dermatologist and cancer unit. I seemed healthy.

Then, in January 1978, only six months after my cancer diagnosis, my father unexpectedly passed away. Harry was either seventy-five or seventy-three, as we weren't sure if his date of birth was 1903 or 1905. One was the date on his immigration papers from Poland, the other the date his family gave him. He preferred 1905, because it made him feel younger, put a spring in his step. Harry would waltz more proudly with his chest puffed out and his straight hair slicked back with the hair product, Vitalis—a word he couldn't pronounce with his Polish-Yiddish accent—so he called it "Witalis." And we constantly teased him about it.

Harry loved driving north on Bayview Avenue when it was still fields of grass, taking us past brand new residential areas like Post Road and the Bridal Path. He would point to a huge fancy home on an enormous treed lot and say, "See that house, it's not mine." Afterwards he took us for apple pie at another of his favourite greasy spoons in a strip-mall on an undeveloped stretch of Eglinton, west of Caledonia.

Because he worked long hours at *the shop*, Harry was often absent but when he was home he was very present for me, listening to me recite memory work of poems over and over from the opposite corner of the room. He wasn't physically affectionate, except in photographs or in public, when he'd yank me indelicately around the neck with his forearm in an attempt at warmth.

At the office with business contacts, he drank Crown Royal, or *schnapps* (as he called the whiskey) but never to excess. Because he often refused his kids' requests for money, I would invent novel ways of extracting twenty-dollar bills from him. Bothered by his demonstrations of anger toward my mother and younger brother, I always tried to please him. Just as Harry tried to please his siblings, who were threatened by any show of love for his own children. The misdeeds of one generation are easily visited on the next, so I vowed that in my own offspring, I would break the cycle of seeking approval whilst ignoring one's own needs.

After his first stroke, Harry had been very upset by the residual handicaps. He went to occupational therapy classes where he made macramé plant hangers to strengthen his small muscle groups, but he loathed being picked up by the Wheeltrans bus. He preferred driving around in his pale blue Cadillac with soft blue plush seats. Its 1977 state-of-the-art features included power windows, a vinyl roof and electrically-adjustable seats. Harry had always wanted a Caddy but bought Oldsmobiles because he didn't want to show off like other nouveau-riche immigrant men. His children had finally convinced him to splurge on one the previous year. He became very depressed seeing it idle in the driveway. His will to live diminished and soon he was gone.

Shiva (the seven-day mourning period after the funeral) was difficult. I had just been dealing with my own mortality and now, for the first time, I was an immediate family member of the deceased. People flocked to my mother's house on

Croydon Road. Harry the joker, the fun dad, was gone. My friends remembered having long, pleasant conversations on the phone with him, then when I asked him who had called, he would say, "Ina-Deena-Enid," meaning either Ina, or Susan, or Enid. I only found out later who had actually rung by speaking to them.

One month later, my sister Lynni and I were booked into a cruise previously planned as a celebration for my recovery from surgery. Although devastated by our recent loss we nevertheless decided to go. She, almost nineteen, and I, almost thirty-one, cherished the opportunity of spending a long stretch of time together. Partying would be a distraction from our sorrow.

The cruise departed from New Orleans, where we listened to jazz and wandered Bourbon Street, then boarded the Russian liner, *MV Odessa*, to disco 'til dawn as it made its way down the Mississippi River to the Gulf of Mexico.

While I practised the art of covering up from the sun, Lynni honed her skills of sun-tanning, unwilling to listen to her big sister's pleas. With me ashore touring Caribbean islands, she overexposed herself and half-fainting, needed to be pulled out of the shower. But we survived. Returning to face the reality of Toronto without Harry, we reassured ourselves by saying he would have preferred we go, rather than lose money by cancelling.

I started back at the office slowly, having been off work for extended periods twice within one year due to unhappy life events. Patients greeted me warmly, listened to my apologies for my absences because of my own illness and my father's death and wanted to carry on as before.

Some people asked more questions wanting to be reassured that I was okay. We continued with business as usual. The rhythm of the work-day became a soothing balm and as the days and months passed, life settled into a more normal pace.

Just when I thought things were settling down, I received a letter in the mail. The envelope was addressed in perfect penmanship, with broad, open European handwriting. Inside was a typewritten white page with a thick black border. It was a lawyer's letter, from Holland.

You have recently written to Koos and Marjanne Eekhout. We are acting on behalf of their estate. You probably have not received notification. They were on the plane that crashed near Tenerife, in the Canary Islands last spring, on March 27, 1977, with their two young children, aged three and two.

Let us remember these wonderful people. They are gone. Only we are left. And their families...

My head began to swim. I read, unable to comprehend the English words. I had sent Christmas greetings to the couple we'd met in the mission hospital in Africa five years earlier. I hadn't heard from them recently, but that was not unusual. The page shook in my hands. I didn't even know they had a second baby. She had tried so hard to get pregnant in Dzodze, Ghana and only conceived when she returned to Holland. Oh my God—they were all dead. Last spring? That was before my surgery. Where had I been all those months? It didn't seem possible. My face was wet.

I sat down and thought about this amazing couple. Koos and Marjanne were gone. Gone, after all the fire and energy they'd put into their missionary work in West Africa.

He, the general practitioner, had been willing to operate by candlelight with a textbook open at the foot of the bed, performing emergency surgery he had never done before, trying to save the life of one mortal in Dzodze.

She, a physiotherapist, had driven across the border into Togo to smuggle back X-ray films so they could print what they only fleetingly saw on the fluoroscope. She had to *dash*, or bribe, the border guards with aspirins which were a rarity there in order to get back into Ghana with her illegal stash of film. They bought screening for the windows of the children's ward to keep out flies and mosquitoes that transmitted bacterial diarrhoea from one dehydrated baby to another, a common occurrence in other mission hospitals.

I recalled in the middle of one night, Koos was jarred awake by the nurse's plea of, "Please, doktah, come quick." He raced up to the operating room and delicately examined the man on the table, whose umbilicus was cut out and his guts wrapped in a sandy, grey cloth. The fetish healing ritual had failed. It was Koos's job to repair the tranced-out man and return him to life. Even Koos couldn't do it. But he certainly tried... all night long.

I remembered how Koos, a staunch Catholic who spoke perfect English, loved to tease and joke and when something went wrong, he was the first to say: *Godverdomme*, and *potverdorie*. (God damn this and God damn that.) I left Dzodze one month later with full command of swear words in Dutch.

One evening, Koos and Marjanne instructed the housekeeper, Millicent Mercy, to prepare the local specialty of *akpleh* and sent her to market to buy the finest goat's meat available. When she presented her creation, I got nauseous looking at it. Koos and Marjanne laughed and he quickly whipped up something else to fill my belly.

In Dzodze, I got to experience this couple's essence and their love of the local people. Their lives were suddenly snuffed out in a plane crash on a holiday they so deserved. They were with the children they had dreamt about during their first two years in Africa and then for another two years after that when Koos refused to leave until a suitable doctor was found to replace him.

No one could replace them.

Awful news seemed to keep coming in those two years. Once again I relied on the regular rhythm and routine of the office to keep me focused, but I was ready for some good times, and some quiet times.

With no recurrence of the cancer and feeling totally well three years after the surgery, my physicians gave me the okay to get pregnant. After one year of trying, I began to get anxious, then suddenly a baby was on the way.

Most of my patients never realized I was pregnant. When I told one of my old guys, Charlie Nelson, that I'd be taking off to have a baby, he was shocked and said, "I thought you were too old for that. I thought you had just put on some weight."

And indeed, I wasn't a huge waddling apparition, as I only gained 20 pounds the entire pregnancy and had a cute little round tummy. I had optimistically assured friends that having a baby wouldn't alter my lifestyle. I could simply put the baby in the bottom drawer of my file cabinet while I continued to see patients.

Childbirth Education in the early '80s promoted natural childbirth, Lamaze for breathing during labour and La Leche for breast feeding. Aiming for as little interference with labour and delivery as safely possible, we felt we were very modern, going where no one had been with childbirth before. Just like these days of celebrity 'bumps' and fashionable SUV strollers, new mothers trot around in Lululemon outfits with Starbucks coffees in their holders, trying to make being a mom trendy and fashionable.

There were certainly no doulas or childbirth assistants and few midwives in those days, but if I wanted good advice about breast feeding, I could ask my mother, who did it many years earlier with all five of her children. So how fashionable was it in the '80s, or now, if my mother was doing it in the '40s and '50s? Maybe each generation has to believe they're re-inventing childbirth and breast feeding.

In the process of finding a locum to look after my practice, I interviewed Emma Silver, but she seemed too careful and meticulous and I worried she would engender anxiety in my patients, so instead I chose her to be my friend and found another woman to care for my patients.

I had hired an excellent secretary who quit at the last minute to repair Persian carpets, so I had to scurry around for a replacement. I stopped work around my due date in early August, expecting to have a Leo baby, but she preferred to be a September Virgo, so I had an entire month to do nothing but walk the dog. I thought I'd never go into labour. When the indicators of the baby's well-being—my blood estriols—began to fall, they wanted to induce me. Just then, my little one started knocking at the door.

In the hours before my daughter's birth, Murphy intervened again and everything that could go wrong in a humorous way, did. On the way down to the Toronto Western Hospital, where I was born and where today they no longer deliver babies, Jonathan and I were stopped by the police for speeding. He didn't believe that I was in labour because I didn't have an enormous belly and when we explained that we were both doctors, he doubted us even more.

Finally arriving at the hospital, Jonathan searched for a parking spot, while I stood in the elevator, doubled over with contractions. At long last, we were settled in a labour room. Jonathan pushed on my sacrum to ease the posterior labour, which sent me sailing across the room. The bed had no brakes and no one could figure out how to fix it. Moving me into another room with a more stable bed, they lost my brightly coloured pillow from home and the loose change we'd collected for the payphones—at the time the only way to announce our new arrival—flew across the delivery room floor.

I used my childbirth exercises, breathing and self-hypnosis techniques all the way through labour and delivery. Each time the nurses approached me to listen to the heart beat, I was in the middle of a contraction, when it was uncomfortable and impossible to hear, so I silently swatted them away. Otherwise labour progressed well, until I was forced to remain flat on the bed for the monitors, so without the benefit of gravity everything slowed down.

The first time I emerged from my hypnotic trance was at the moment of her birth, when the nurses placed her on my chest. To their astonishment, I gleefully uttered, "It's a mother-fuckin' girl!" She was tiny, about five and a half pounds and looked like a little old man, just like Harry. We had already decided to name the baby after him, his Hebrew name being *Zvi*, meaning deer, so we swapped one quick animal for another and she became an *Arye*, or lion. We francophonized and feminized the boy's name Ariel to become Arielle. And so she came to be.

We were thrilled with her, but totally unprepared for the chaos a first baby can bring into an adult household. I had been well-prepared for labour and delivery, but not for actually dealing with a newborn. It wasn't about how to hold or wrap or change or bathe her. It was about problem-solving. What to do when she was fed and changed and warm and *still crying*. There were no answers and no textbooks to provide them. What worked one day never worked the next. I adored the infant but was frustrated with infant care.

By six and a half weeks post-partum, I needed to feel a sense of accomplishment not provided by changing dirty diapers. I decided I needed to return to work. We very carefully chose Priscilla, a wonderful, capable Philippine nanny to love and care for our precious jewel, so I could happily return to my patients.

It was difficult leaving Arielle at home, but it would have been harder to stay. I was frustrated pumping breast milk and racing home to feed her at the end of a long day, but as she began smiling back at me, irritations drained. It was all worthwhile. How naive I was to think I could take her to work with me. My life had indeed changed, but for the better, with a sweet little munchkin to keep me busy. It is unthinkable not to have her in my life and yet, if my rebellious nature hadn't been provoked by the challenge of getting pregnant after the cancer, I might have been too busy partying and procrastinating until I was too old to deal with the rigours of child-rearing. Somehow the cancer provided focus, helping move me toward my priority.

CHAPTER 12

Farming Days

As a new immigrant to Canada from Poland, my father worked long hours for many years. When he died at 73 (or 75), the five of us inherited a substantial sum of money. My two younger siblings, Lawrie and Lynni, were still living at home with our mother Hellie. Jonathan and I spent many Friday night dinners with them, so the four of us became very close. Lynni, who was 20, decided to use her inheritance as a down-payment on a cottage on Lake Simcoe. Soon afterwards, my brother Lawrie and I pooled our portions to buy a working farm near Cannington Ontario, less than a half hour from Lynni's cottage.

Lawrie was our baby brother, six years younger than me, six years older than Lynni. I had taken care of him from birth, changing his diapers, holding his hand when he precociously tried to walk. Strong-minded and curious, Lawrie had a nasty temper and was always making trouble at home. My mother first introduced the phrase, *Fung Nisht Un* (don't start up), in an effort to keep things peaceful around Lawrie. If he was playing quietly by himself, we were supposed to leave him be. If he wanted something, we had to give it to him, lest he start throwing things in angry tantrums. At the family's summer cottage near Beaverton Ontario, we glued together a glass lampshade that Lawrie had smashed with a shoe before my father came up on the weekend. Mediating between Lawrie and my father became my full-time job.

When Lawrie was 20, he was arrested in Italy for carrying drugs across the border from France. He claimed the small amount of marijuana he carried was for personal use and that the heroin belonged to his travelling buddy, who was mysteriously released. My father was furious. Eager to defuse the situation, I flew to Italy. When the Italian court gave Lawrie the maximum sentence of seven years—perhaps sending a message to other foreigners involved in drugs—I was devastated. I had gone all that way and seemingly accomplished nothing.

Lawrie was livid with me for coming to the trial but asked me to stop in Amsterdam on my way home to retrieve a $1000 bill hidden under the floorboards of his apartment, where, unbeknownst to my parents, he'd been dealing drugs for a year. I met his landlady, got into his flat, searched for the cash and surrendered the apartment, knowing I had to keep it all a secret from the family. Upon my return, my father was outraged when my only news was the lawyer's request for more money to act on Lawrie's behalf. Six weeks later, Lawrie was unexpectedly released. He insisted that my presence in Italy had made no difference.

Though my contributions were never acknowledged, it was important to me that I had tried. As hard as it was, I was willing to do anything for Lawrie in my role as caregiver. I was frustrated when he disrespected limits, yet loved his rebellious side—no matter how angry he made me, I still adored him. The words of a song kept playing over and over in my head: *He ain't heavy, he's my brother.*

Why was it so important to mediate between Lawrie and my father? Why had I feared their anger? Harry 'took off the strap' to Lawrie when he was little, attempting to control him, but he never hit my mother or the rest of us. It was only Lawrie who acted out physically. Eventually I came to understand that my mother's old-fashioned rules about women pleasing men, gaining their approval and keeping things calm and pleasant, were with me still.

When the farm proposal came up six years later, Lawrie had matured into a tall, muscular, blonde, long-haired and independent-minded adult. He had completed two years of a BA program in agriculture at Guelph, but had gotten bored. Rather than do more book learning, he wanted to put his knowledge into practice. A farm was the perfect venue.

Though Jon and I were still child-free at that point, some of our friends told us we were foolish to embark on such a big venture with Lawrie. I was optimistic, however, and believed in my brother's smarts, physical strength and know-how. I figured Jon, who had Lawrie's respect, could act as a buffer if necessary. Looking back, I see I was trying once again to mediate between my father and Lawrie. Harry had left all this money and I felt responsible for ensuring Lawrie's share would be spent wisely.

The plan was for Lawrie to live there during the week as a full-time farmer. Jon and I went up for leisurely weekends as 'gentle-person farmers'. No matter how exhausted I was on a Friday night after work, I insisted upon getting into the car and heading up the back roads in the pitch black, in order to crawl into my farm bed and wake up the next morning to fresh air and total silence. Sitting with a coffee on the wide porch overlooking the fields, I was soothed by the heavenly stillness.

That first year we worked hard making the farmhouse homey and comfortable. During the week, Lawrie made lists of jobs he expected us to do when we arrived. After a hard week of practising medicine, we ended up working again on the farm on the weekends.

An 1860s red brick building, the house had been owned by one family for generations. They had upgraded the utilities, wiring in electricity to replace gas lamps, installed central heating ducts, yet left the huge old wood-stove in the large country kitchen for ancillary heat. A new well was connected to indoor plumbing, but a red-painted hand-pump remained outside over the original well. Mechanically, the house had been brought into the twentieth century, but aesthetically it had not. The windows were cracked, leaking cold air in winter and heat in summer; the ceilings were splitting. The wainscoting was badly painted, the floors creaky. All the old charm remained but had languished over time. Lawrie decided to fix it all himself. What would take a construction crew months to tear out and restore to its original beauty, Lawrie believed he could do faster by being up there alone.

He soon demolished the kitchen and the bathroom. He loaded the back of his white Chevy pick-up with debris to take to the dump and returned to the farm with supplies of wood and other materials, back and forth, by himself all week. Everything was torn apart simultaneously, leaving dust everywhere. By balancing one end of a huge sheet of drywall on a ladder and lifting the other end with his strong, ectomorphic body, he was able to re-do the ceilings by himself. Jonathan and I had to move out of our original cosy bedroom into another huge room above the summer kitchen. We tried to say no, but Lawrie always had a good argument for doing things his way, so we relented. He was smart and omni-competent, but his dope-smoking meant he inhabited a very laid-back place. Weekend after weekend, we drove out to our beloved get-away only to find more sections of the house ripped open.

We fixed up the barn to accommodate a herd of eight heifers, which Lawrie learned to care for and breed expertly, sending their offspring to market when they were plump and round. His brilliant mind constantly hatched new plans to build a berm into the side of a hill, renovate the barn further, extend water out to it, or take down some trees and plant others. He also wanted to expand the crops into money-making ventures. We listened politely, knowing it was not all possible and tried to whittle his dreams down to realistic goals.

When the weather was hot, we trekked over to Lynni's cottage to visit with her friends, swim, boat and play frisbee. On fall days, Lynni and her buddies came to help us bring in the hay and plough the fields under for winter wheat with our shiny, green John Deere tractor. After the chores were done, we barbequed delectable steak, freshly-slaughtered from the locker service in Cannington, or pigged out on chicken Savoyard. We boiled live lobster and charred hot dogs and marshmallows over an open fire pit on the back forty. One night we had an enormous party with speakers blaring outside and danced our brains out. It was lively, crazy, so much fun.

Lawrie's friends slept over during the week when we weren't there and our friends stayed overnight on the weekends. But his friends also arrived randomly at any time and were constantly smoking dope. Laughter and deep, intense discussion ensued. I wandered in and out of the conversation at will as I performed indoor tasks in the house, but had to find some calm spot away from the gang to quietly read a book.

As time passed, I found it hard to have so many people around all the time, missing the privacy I was used to at home in the city. Lawrie liked to stay up half the night and slept in much later than I did. He was cranky when finally he did wake up. We had different long-term goals for the farm, which we hadn't clarified beforehand. Doubts crept in. 'The best-laid plans of mice and men, gang aft a-gley...' Robbie Burns' poem kept repeating in my brain. But we persevered because I loved being in the country for all the fun times.

Renovations could proceed at their own pace, but caring for the herd was an ongoing responsibility. After calving, all of the heifers required vitamin injections. Most were cooperative and got their needles out in the fields. Only Lucy had eluded the shot and we knew she would be tough to deal with. A dark brown cow with deep determined black eyes, she tended to stay away from the pack and we all steered clear of her. We didn't have a proper enclosure for the animals in the barn, so we created a make-shift pen out of some gates we held in place to confine her.

From our work with kids, Jonathan and I were experienced at giving shots quickly, but as Jon stabbed her, Lucy bolted and took off out of the barn with the syringe still in her backside, knocking over the fence I had been supporting and taking me down with it. I crashed backwards onto the barn stairs, then onto the floor, as Lucy galloped over me, hoofs landing either side of my body. All I remember is her gigantic brown underbelly flying over me in slow motion. I was six weeks pregnant. I'd had to wait three years after my melanoma surgery, so I was in a doubly precarious state. All I could think of was the baby. It hurt to breathe, but I was alive. Aghast and terrified, Jonathan and Lawrie came running over to help me get up and hobble back to the house.

That was it for me. I felt overwhelmed, frustrated and scared. What had started out as fun had become dangerous, aggravating and expensive. The venture was no longer a joy but a huge burden. There was no stopping Lawrie in any direction. He planned to take delivery of more cattle at the same time my baby was due. I had to put on the brakes. Saying no to Lawrie would be hard—I loved him dearly and feared his temper—but now I had no choice. I could no longer afford his dreams.

Jonathan and I wanted to be on firm ground, so we asked Lawrie to come by our house in the city. I was nervous and I'm sure he knew something was up. We sat down in the kitchen and tried to explain calmly that the farm was no longer working for us. We had a baby coming who would need our attention. We told him we had to put the farm up for sale.

He suddenly stood up, yelling at us that we didn't know what we were talking about; what we were saying was impossible; we were plotting against him. How could we deprive him of his full-time home and career? What would he do with his life? He insisted we weren't being fair. We tried to explain, but he couldn't understand our point of view. He stomped out the back door and drove off in his white pick-up. I had no idea what he would do with his rage. I was scared he would torch the farm or set fire to our house. That night I couldn't sleep.

I hated the thought of giving up walks in the fields, treks through the woods, rhubarb picking and vegetable planting. I loved watching Lawrie's Afghan dog, Sharif, barrel around the barnyard. I loved the break from the city. I loved going into town to shop for dinner and instead of finding what we had planned to eat, returning with whatever was available. I loved watching the heifers in the fields with their new calves...

After several sleepless nights and days of hearing nothing, we finally got a call from Lawrie saying he'd arranged for a real estate agent to meet us at the farm. To this day, I have no idea how it came about. The meeting was tense, but with a strangely united front, the three of us managed to convince the agent to list the property for more than she suggested. Even though the renovations were incomplete, we wanted to re-coup our investment, plus benefit from the increase in property value over the past four years. The beautiful property sold quickly. We also managed to make some money at an auction on the front lawn selling furniture, beds, linens, kitchen supplies, farm equipment, tools and the green John Deere. With huge regrets and a lot of tears, we eventually got through the trauma of the sale.

Lawrie rented an apartment in the city and started trading stocks. We rarely saw him but did catch up with him at Lynni's cottage and managed to stay on reasonably friendly terms even though we were never as connected as we'd been before the farm purchase. I felt sad about what had transpired, but was convinced I had done my best. I felt guilty about dragging Jonathan into my *mishega'as* (craziness) with my brother, but he had seemed a willing and loving partner in the adventure. I realized that although I had originally made a rather glib decision to go to medical school—choosing it as one path that did not lead to teaching—I had unconsciously chosen a field that exactly matched my natural tendencies for caretaking. Whether it had anything to do with my birth order as the middle child or just my innate nature, I had picked well, even become passionate about my choice. But I was beginning to see that I would have to contain some of those tendencies or risk burning myself out—not only with Lawrie but with my patients, also. I needed to learn to look after myself and my own immediate family. My days of rescuing my brother were over.

Meanwhile, my younger, wiser sister Lynni carried on with her cottage all to herself, managing it however she pleased. She turned it into a very comfortable, antique-filled, up-to-date, year-round home where we were always welcome, even with our new baby.

Over time, I missed the farm intensely. When our daughter Arielle turned three, Jonathan and I bought our own stretch of fields near Cobourg in the Shelter Valley. This time we hired people to do the necessary repairs so we could relax on the weekends. We hung wallpaper but I was otherwise content with the condition of the farmhouse. We rented the land out to a local farmer. His cows were not allowed to graze around the pond in order to leave it *au naturel* with a few seedlings on its banks. This time we didn't get a full-sized John Deere tractor but couldn't resist buying a small riding mower. I would drive up late on Friday from the city, awakening next morning to sunshine on the front lawn before playing in the backyard on the swing with Arielle. We entertained friends when we chose to and had privacy at other times. We luxuriated in long, slow walks into the back forty. My blissful visits to the country had resumed.

My only regret was that I never invited Lawrie to visit. I couldn't bear to listen to a litany of suggestions about what to do with the place, which for him would have simply been innocent dreams. I couldn't take the risk of getting hooked again. We spent four glorious years at this farm until it finally had to be sold due to an enormous heartbreak—the dissolution of my marriage.

CHAPTER 13

Larry and Lawrie

Throughout eventful years of my cancer surgery, my father's death and running the farm with my brother, one huge constant in my life was my medical practice. As busy as it was, it kept me focused and grounded, as if my patients were keeping me sane. When Dr Da Silva lost the provincial election in 1981, he decided to embark upon a psychiatry residency, which meant we would no longer share a General Practice office. I moved to a one-person suite down the hall, an easy task compared to the upsets in my private life. My new office was bright with a floor-to-ceiling window overlooking the inner city back lanes. Patients were happy to enjoy a new milieu and I was thrilled to make all office decisions independently. Shortly thereafter, I took off on maternity leave.

I returned six weeks post-partum to find the office in chaos. A locum had been seeing my patients but none of the paperwork was done thanks to a randomly-hired replacement for my regular secretary. I was in serious need of good office help and asked anyone who would listen, including patients. One of my favourites, Fuge, a musician in a cabaret act in Toronto called *The Time Twins*, suggested her buddy Larry Stanley. She claimed Larry was bright and funny and needed a day job to supplement his evening music gigs. His only relevant experience was working in a downtown group-home for troubled youth.

We met at the office and conversed easily for half an hour. He was friendly, medium height, skinny, with a receding brown hairline and a twinkle in his green/blue eyes. Although it occurred to me I should wait for someone with a bit of medical background, I was charmed and hired him on the spot. He came in several times to learn the office systems, quickly picking up details of filing, phones, referrals, billing, banking and bookkeeping. There was nothing I could throw at him that he didn't respond to well. Later on, I even taught him how to syringe wax from people's ears and how to weigh squirming infants. He was a brilliant choice and started out working three days a week.

One day early on, I went to call a patient in from the waiting room only to find her and Larry embroiled in a deep conversation about music which I was loathe to interrupt. She explained that she was also a musician and knew him from way back; they had performed on stage together.

Larry soon figured out how to book my schedule perfectly and learned to screen phone calls so I had very few people to contact at the end of the day. Patients loved his spontaneous wacky wit and because they felt so relaxed with him, they'd open up on the phone so he often knew more about them than I did. One patient was shy about her female parts and would giggle when she told him she had a problem 'down there', sure he knew exactly what she meant.

Jonathan and I started to attend his gigs around town at The Brunswick House, Free Times Café and C'est What? Loving his keyboard work and the songs he wrote, we bought many of his cassette tapes. We met his friends and partied together. Larry smoked, drank a lot of scotch (Chivas Regal was his favourite) and he joked endlessly. He later joined us for Arielle's birthday parties and met my relatives so he became part of our family. He said it was the best day-job he'd ever had.

Larry had grown up on a farm in Lloydminster, Saskatchewan, so he totally understood the hassles of country properties. I shared my farm-related woes with him: my upset about Lawrie's plans for the farm, the incident with Lucy and my conclusion that we had to sell. I confided my feelings of guilt about making Lawrie move back to the city, putting an end to his glorious days alone in the country with his Afghan dog and the heifers. He was totally supportive of me and turned out to be *my* psychotherapist.

One day, Larry buzzed me on the intercom and with a tone of urgency, told me to take a phone call, whispering that it was a policeman on the line. I excused myself from the patient and heart in mouth, took the call.

"Are you Dr Sharon Baltman?"

"Yes."

"Is your thirteen-month-old daughter Arielle in the care of a nanny named Ruby?"

"Yes. Is she OK? What happened?" I cried into the phone.

"Well, there's been a bit of an accident," he said slowly.

"Is she OK?" I screeched.

"Her foot got caught in a TTC bus door, but for clarification, she was taken to hospital."

"Just tell me if she's alive and well. Where is she?" I gasped.

"They've sent her home. You can meet them there," was all he would tell me.

In a totally calm voice, Larry offered to cancel my day of patients due to an emergency at home and suggested I call home before leaving. Ruby, a pleasant 30-ish Guyanese woman recently hired to replace Arielle's treasured first nanny, answered and acted as if nothing had happened. She told me she was carrying Arielle off the bus, when the door closed on one of her little feet. I didn't understand that if Ruby was still standing on the step that activated the door to open, how the door could possibly close? How could the foot of a thirteen-month-old be so far behind the two of them?

I drove home, my heart pounding with anxiety and guilt. When I finally entered the house on Lawton Boulevard, Ruby greeted me warmly as usual. Arielle was sitting quietly in her highchair, stuffing macaroni and cheese into her mouth. I was relieved that all was well. I listened to the story over and over and to this day, still can't comprehend what happened.

I was angry, terrified, confused. I had left my precious daughter in the hands of someone who might have let her be harmed. I had allowed my need to work to supersede the safety of my offspring. My desire for a sense of organization and some feeling of accomplishment from seeing patients had put my child at risk. I knew my patients' needs were not more important than her well-being. I wondered if I should give up my practice to stay home. I had spent all those years studying to be a doctor and now I might have to leave that behind to ensure the safety of my innocent little sweetie… I was facing the classic dilemma of the working mother: *What to do? How to proceed?*

When I calmed down, I concluded that realistically I could not stay home full-time, as I would go mad conversing with a one-year-old all day. I needed the stimulation of work to keep my brain active. Rightly or wrongly, our rationale was to blame the nanny. Jonathan and I set out to find someone else who would do the job more carefully. It had taken a long time to find Ruby and now we were at it again. Larry listened to my stories about the exorbitant agency fees and helped me screen applicants. He made me laugh with his inane jokes about the difficult situation, even composing a song titled: *Babysitters on French Toast*. After many long, tedious weeks of searching, we hired Cécile, a Swiss twenty-something who was smart, conscientious and independent. She turned out to be a joy to have around and even took care of Shuvi, our golden retriever. Like Larry, she soon became part of our little family.

In early 1985, after working together for about three years, Larry got a call informing him that his brothers had been involved in a terrible car crash in Saskatchewan. His younger brother Vernon had been killed and his other brother Gordon was in critical condition. Larry needed to fly home for the funeral to support his mother in her grief. He had no credit cards, so he charged his flight to my Visa and was gone.

I missed him terribly and the office reverted to chaos. Patients missed him, worried about his well-being and wondered if he'd ever return. I got temporary help, but no one could reassure patients, protect me and organize the entire office like he did. I had endless phone calls to return; bookings were mixed up, patients upset. One month later, grieving and crest-fallen, Larry returned. In short order, the office was ship-shape once again. The golden voice had resurfaced.

In the months following his trauma, Larry and I went for long dinners sharing intimate details of our lives. He talked about his brothers and his piano-teaching mom whom he adored. He told me how she could never get him to learn to read music—he only wanted to play by ear. He loved his family but couldn't tolerate the small-town mentality of rural Saskatchewan over the long-term. We spoke about his passionate spirituality that was not part of organized religion. We compared my little Ontario farm to Larry's family's huge working farm operation out west, run by his eldest brother,

Ken. Our relationship deepened and we became very close buddies.

In July 1985, about one year after Lawrie and I sold the farm, Jon and I received a call at our new farm telling us that Jonathan's father had died of lung cancer. He was in his seventies and had been ill for a while, but we hadn't expected him to die so soon. We raced back to the city for the funeral the next day. Upon arriving home in Toronto, we took another call summoning us to my mother's house on Croydon Road. The last time I was called to the family home was in 1978 when my father died.

We arranged for a babysitter from up the road to stay with Arielle while we went to my mother's. On that hot sticky July evening, we walked up the winding path to Hellie's house, full of dread. It didn't sound good. I told Jonathan I couldn't take anything more at that point. I had just been diagnosed with Grave's Disease and was already hyper from the excess thyroid hormone in my system. I was hot all the time, had lost a lot of weight and was anxious and depressed. I had just started treatment with propylthiouracil (PTU) to cool down my thyroid gland, but it hadn't done its job yet.

Upon entering the house, I heard the words: "Lawrie's gone."

"Gone where?" I asked.

"He did it. Lawrie took his own life," my older brother Zel said.

The tears burst out. I was sobbing, my chest heaving and heavy. I moved slowly from Lynni, to Rena, back to Zel and then to Hellie, as Jonathan followed behind me. We were weeping and hugging and holding each other as one. My mother was a wreck. She kept asking where she had gone wrong. Was there something more she could have done for Lawrie? We were all in shock. We couldn't believe it. *How could it be true? How could he have done this? At thirty-one years old? Was he really that unhappy? What could we have done? Was it my fault? Should I have sent him to yet another psychiatrist?*

But then from my mother, our *Rock*, came the words: "It's nobody's fault. We all did what we could for him. Each and every one of us."

She was right. We all knew he was unhappy. Hellie had bent over backwards for Lawrie all his life. When he was five years old, she walked up and down the hall at 2 am with him crying with stomach pains that years later doctors discovered were due to peptic ulcers, a rare diagnosis in children at the time. When he was young, she took him to a psychologist to try to understand his uncontrollable temper. No one could help. As an adult, I had sent him to two different psychiatrists. One said he didn't need therapy. The second Lawrie said wasn't smart enough for him. What more was there to do?

Nowadays he might be diagnosed with ADHD or 'oppositional defiant behaviour disorder', but such diagnoses weren't made in the '60s when he was in trouble. So later in his life he self-medicated with dope and alcohol. After the farm was sold, he tried to make a living on the stock market. He was too proud to admit defeat, so when his money ran out he ended his life.

The funeral was planned for the next afternoon. The next morning, in our grief, my siblings and I attended the funeral service for Jonathan's father. As I was openly sobbing leaving the funeral home with the immediate family after the service, one of the attendants attempted to reassure me. "Let's hope you don't have to come back here for a very long time."

"Lawrence Baltman is my brother. He's in this building right now and I'll be back for his funeral this afternoon." Crying even harder, I somehow made my way into the limousine heading for the cemetery for the first time that day. My head was screeching with pain. No painkillers could calm it.

I did return to the funeral home for the afternoon service, but recall nothing except the trip back to the cemetery and the enormous pain of watching my mother's agony as she said good-bye to her son. It was so unnatural, horrible, to see Hellie so distraught. But she soon calmed herself, thereby settling us down.

I was devastated. How could all these things be happening at the same time? My father-in-law dying, my brother dying, my thyroid out of control? It was huge. When I felt down, I cried. Jonathan cried with me. We tried to protect Arielle and act normally with her, but it was not easy. She knew I was sad. We told her that her *Zadie* Nit-Nat had died and so had her

Uncle Lawrie. She wouldn't see them again. She didn't understand, but I didn't understand either.

Shiva was intense. For seven days, our beloved home on Croydon Road was packed with family and friends. People we hadn't seen for years came to pay their respects, console us. I remember at times attempting to comfort them: "He was always so troubled. At least he's at peace. Now he can rest."

Jon and I went back and forth between the two *shiva* houses. It was exhausting. I tried to get some sleep in one of the bedrooms upstairs, but new people were constantly arriving who wanted to console me. And every day another friend or relative sent a huge catered meal to fill our bellies. I couldn't eat, but it was part of the custom to sit down at the table for dinner and try to swallow some morsels. The ritual served as a diversion from the pain.

Unanswered questions remained. *He must have known that we would do anything for him, why hadn't he asked for more help? Was his life really so dreadful? Why didn't we notice his pain?*

One of my colleagues, a psychiatrist, offered to sit down, as a friend, at the dining room table with my immediate family and let us air our queries. He said he couldn't provide answers, but hoped that by talking together we might get some peace. Some of us were more silent than others but we all listened intently. Just to gather and focus was healing. It was enormously helpful to hear my siblings' feelings and concerns. We were all grateful for his help.

Then after just a week, we had to return to our lives. Looking around I saw that everything else had gone on without us. Nothing in the outside world had changed, while everything in my life had. Nothing would ever be the same for me. I knew I would get through it, but it wouldn't be easy. I could only take it one day at a time. Along with all my wonderfully supportive family and friends, Larry was there for me. But Larry was special. He knew exactly what I was going through: only six months down the road he was going through the loss of a brother all over again—with me. We talked and laughed and cried. Our connection tightened. And how interesting that I had never noticed the similarities between Larry and Lawrie: born seven months apart, both skinny, fair-haired, smart, interesting, off-the-wall and both loved their booze or drug of choice. Larry became my surrogate brother—but not for long.

In 1986, I changed direction in my practice, no longer requiring a receptionist. By so doing, I lost my personal psychotherapist, but Larry and I remained friends, continuing our long dinners and wild, crazy weekend parties that always included Jonathan and a whole host of Larry's assorted friends. Because Larry never discussed his sexuality or mentioned any partners, over the years Jonathan and I somehow concluded he was asexual. We were totally wrong.

Soon after he stopped working for me, Larry told me without a shred of embarrassment, that at the baths he had met Will, the love of his life. They were great together. Will was even more spiritual than Larry and their connection was intense. Will had mental health issues which he labelled his 'astral travelling', but Larry managed to keep him grounded. Will started to paint and created huge canvases in oil of brightly-coloured flowers for all of us. As we had done before, Will followed Larry to his gigs around town. We all sang along with Larry's compositions like *Public Sex*, *Café Society*, *Daddy's Little Jewel*, and *Genuine Love*. During the applause after every song, Will howled like a wild wolf. Larry smiled glowingly.

It was the 1980s and the Human Immunodeficiency Virus was rampant in gay communities. I had many HIV-positive patients in my area of town, but did not specialize in it as many of my colleagues did. Research on a vaccine could not keep up with the mutations of which the virus was capable. Every day we heard about someone new being infected or ill or dying. It was shocking.

Soon we found out that Will had become ill with full-blown AIDS. Larry quit both his day and night jobs to care for him. At first in Will's tiny, gloomy apartment on George Street, then later at Larry's more spacious place on Lansdowne Avenue. I went to visit them in their seedy neighbourhood which felt like *Crack Alley*, just north of the mental hospital, formerly known as the 'loony-bin at 999 Queen Street'. In that high-ceilinged, one-room pad with a bedroom at the back, Larry nursed Will patiently and lovingly. It was during that period that Larry's mother, and then his eldest brother, Ken, died. So by the time Will passed away, Larry was a bag of bones well-preserved by Scotch. He still managed to throw a huge party as a wake for Will on Lansdowne, but the howling was absent.

After Will's death, Larry had nothing to keep him busy, so he drank even more. We worried about his health. Then he began to write songs in Will's memory, like *Don't Say You're Alone,* slowly began to perform again and soon came back to life. He returned to health care, working frenetically as a community home-care coordinator and loving it. He moved out of Lansdowne into an unrenovated warehouse with an iron-gated freight elevator at King and Parliament. He lived in a huge open room without doors, a ladder leading up to a loft bed. In one corner was an altar to Will with lit candles, coloured love birds and other Will-phernalia. In the open space, even the bathroom had only half-walls, so when Larry sat on the throne he could see Will's splashes of colour in his paintings hung on the wall right up to the twenty-foot ceiling.

When his family farm in Saskatchewan was sold, Larry inherited some money and was planning to treat himself to a condo and explore new creative areas in his life. By that point, he and I were only meeting up around twice a year for dinner. In December 1999, I called and left him a message to contact me about setting up our annual birthday celebration. The next thing I heard two months later was a message from Joseph, a total stranger, calling to say that Larry was in Toronto Hospital in serious condition, about to be moved into a private room with a morphine drip.

I raced down to the hospital and there he was: lying in a blue hospital gown, in pain, coughing and struggling to breathe with oxygen prongs in his nose. But his bright eyes were still understanding and smiling at jokes made about sneaking Scotch and chocolate into the hospital for him.

The next day, on February 3, 2000 he died at the age of forty-five, two days after the diagnosis of lung cancer was made. Now my surrogate brother was gone. But Larry didn't want a wake. "A party would be nice. At my *shiva,* you can sip Chivas for me."

I wrote a 'Lives Lived' column about him for the *Globe and Mail* and then read it at 'Larry's Party', a musical tribute held at Clinton's Tavern two months later. I heard from people who had known him years and years ago, letters saying they remembered what a wonderful person he was. Everyone loved

Larry. I feel privileged to have had him in my life and in such an intense way.

Larry taught me a lot in our years together. He taught me to celebrate every step of the way. When I found a buyer for my medical practice and I didn't want to rejoice too soon in case the agreement didn't go through, he told me, "It's never too early to celebrate. You can't wait until it's a done deal. Party now, you can always party again later." And Larry joked about everything. One evening, with his friend Richard, they made hysterically funny puns about every single stop along the Toronto subway line. And we never would have met if it hadn't been for Fuge, who had hooked me up with him. She was another musician who died of cancer at a very young age, long before Larry left us.

I still miss Larry and wonder what he would have to say about things now. At my age he's starting to feel like a dream that never really happened. It was so long ago, but I still cry when I think of him, proving to me he was real. On one occasion, I went to listen to one of his tapes, to hear his voice again, and there was only silence. The cassettes had deteriorated so the sound had disappeared, just like Larry had. But I am reassured that his buddies are currently trying to put his songs into digital format to bring them back to life so his sultry, dulcet tones are never silenced again.

And of course I miss Lawrie. Every day. So hard to imagine that his life was over at age thirty-one. He could have been so much, done so much. My daughter Arielle is around the same age as Lawrie was when he died and she's only beginning her life.

Without either Lawrie or Larry in my life, the one constant that continued to ground me throughout all my travels and travails was my professional practice.

CHAPTER 14

The Big Switch

In early 1984, while Larry was still at the front desk of my general practice, I became more interested in my patients' psychological and emotional lives. The endless variety of human behaviour fascinated me. My training in this area had included studying general psychiatric theory in medical school, shadowing family doctors and psychiatrists doing psychotherapy in my clerkship year and working for one month on an in-patient psychiatry hospital ward during my rotating internship. My skills consisted of listening to the patient and 'doing no harm', as stated in the Hippocratic Oath we took at graduation.

I began spending more hours doing counselling and psychotherapy. Rather than hearing tiny snippets of problems during rushed office visits, I gave patients the opportunity to request half-hour sessions to slowly de-brief and sort through complicated, sometimes painful, life events. These patients did not require the expertise of psychiatrists because they did not have major mental health diagnoses such as schizophrenia or psychosis. They were experiencing stress in their every-day lives and needed help.

I listened carefully while they poured their hearts out, getting to know them, forging a bond. Patients felt unburdened and supported. I enjoyed what I thought of as 'Primary Care Psychotherapy for the Walking Wounded'.

Long ago I had left emergency work to follow patients' progress beyond a first visit; now I was moving from general practice to even more intense individual care. At the same time, there were practical considerations behind my desire to change direction. I was dealing with a huge patient load, the constant pressure of sick kids 'going bad' easily and adults with acute illnesses like heart attacks and pneumonia. Looking after my three-year-old daughter, a farm in the country, a dog and a house in the city, was exhausting. I was keen to simplify things, decrease my stress-load and devote more attention to Arielle.

I did not return to school to complete a psychiatry degree, or do psychoanalytic training, so in order to expand my knowledge base, I took courses in Gestalt Therapy and Transactional Analysis (TA), which were the rage in non-Freudian psychotherapy circles in the '80s. Gestalt focuses on awareness of the individual's experience in the present moment and TA explains how people function by describing three components of the self: how the 'Parent, Adult and Child' of each person interacts with similar components in the other. As well, I enrolled in extension courses in psychoanalytic theory and practice at the Toronto Psychoanalytic Society when it was on Price Street in Rosedale. I also attended their Friday evening presentations which psychoanalysed popular movies.

I soon realized that I also needed a 'supervisor', an experienced senior clinician with whom I could confidentially share details of psychotherapy sessions in order to carefully examine what went on in the consulting room, learn from the interactions and ensure quality of care for the patient. The consulting room provides too much privacy to be allowed to remain unexamined without checks and balances.

Dr Anne Alonso of Harvard Medical School's Department of Psychiatry defines optimal 'psychotherapy supervision' as 'one in which the supervisor is focused primarily on the clinical and professional development of the supervisee. The supervisor, in effect, must listen with a clinician's ear and speak with a teacher's mouth.'

I had heard about a New Zealander, Dr Cameron, a talented and humane psychiatrist working in downtown Toronto. I referred some GP patients to her for psychiatric consultations and all returned with rave reviews so I called and we met at her office on Elm Street. She was energetic, dressed entirely in black, with short brown hair, twinkling eyes and funky high-heeled boots. From the first meeting, we were on a first-name basis.

"I do a lot of supervision of residents at Toronto Western," she explained in her Kiwi accent. "I really enjoy it. Your work as a general practitioner would give me a totally different point of view on psychotherapy. It'll be fascinating." Thereafter, I engaged her services as my supervisor and we set up regular monthly sessions.

Rowena always had the most amazing insights into my patients. She suggested letting one patient adjust her medication dosage in order to stabilize her own depressive symptoms, which worked beautifully. Another woman I was working with thought she was a lesbian and needed to leave her husband. Rowena listened patiently to the details, then said: "She's not gay. She's just afraid of leaving, so she's looking for an excuse." Subsequently the woman divorced her husband and continued to see men.

One day in her office, I finally confessed: "It's hard for me to admit I don't know how to handle certain situations."

"That's exactly why you're coming here."

"But then you come up with the most obvious solutions."

"Sometimes I do, but it's easy for me to sit back and draw conclusions when you've done all the hard work with the patient. I easily end up looking brilliant," she replied.

"But I feel stupid when I miss something."

"That's the learning process and that's what we're doing here. I also gain insights from your perspective as a GP…"

I finally realized I was paying her to listen to my insecurities. During my years of studying and practising medicine, the pressure to be perfect was enormous. You weren't allowed to make errors and if you did, you were expected to cover them up: the bizarre old un-funny joke that doctors 'bury their mistakes'. Whenever past mentors had made mistakes, they would hide them rather than learn from them, or use them to teach a lesson. I finally had a venue to express my slip-ups and doubts and try to rectify them. It was refreshing.

Some sessions were spent dealing not only with my difficulties with patients, but also with my own personal relationships and family issues. When Lawrie died, Rowena helped me understand what he might have been going through and listened to my guilt feelings about him not receiving the help he needed.

I watched her life choices, too, as she moved her office into her home, using a beautiful living room with fireplace as a consulting room and the front hall as a waiting room. She later moved house a second time, digging out her basement to create yet another fabulous home-office. Once, when Rowena was upset, we left for coffee on the Danforth and spent the hour talking through her personal ennui. I was a bit confused and later asked her about boundaries. I'd come to her for supervision of my work with patients and to talk about my difficulties as a therapist. Sometimes we'd talk about my personal problems and other times about hers.

"Is all of this okay?" I finally asked.

"It's a very complex process," she said. "I see it more as a consultation which leaves us room to discuss all sorts of matters in which we each have different levels of expertise. The most important factor is that both of us are comfortable with the process and if not, then we need to discuss it." Although the standard recommendation is to change supervisors periodically, Rowena and I continue our regular consultations to this day.

At first, I started booking my GP patients with emotional difficulties at the end of a day of seeing physically-ill people. I enjoyed the slower pace and patients benefited from having a safe venue to deal with their lives in an open, emotional way; speaking about their depression, anxieties, relationships, fears and phobias. The problem was that I often ran late with my physically-ill patients, which meant keeping already anxious people waiting for long periods of time. I also found myself totally exhausted from the day's work, barely able to listen carefully and respond to their needs.

Then I tried seeing them before the start of my day when I was still fresh and on time, but GP patients noticed my car in the lot and knocked at the locked door, or phoned the office for a prescription. Such distractions interfered with the concentration necessary for psychotherapy; both patient and doctor ended up frustrated.

Next, I tried booking all my GP patients on three days of the week and then spending one full day on psychotherapy. I brought Shuvi, our golden retriever, to sit quietly at my feet while patients worked out their difficulties. They loved having him around and he often sighed loudly after extreme moments. He always sensed the break at lunchtime, jumping up to bring me his leash for a walk on Church Street.

I finally achieved the slower tempo and the deeper connection, so that both patient and I felt satisfied. But then GP patients started discovering me in the office on that day. They would ambush me in the hall on my way in with the dog, bringing sick children with fevers or asking for test results. Larry attempted to educate them otherwise, but to no avail. Chaos soon resumed.

I loved the work and the satisfaction it gave me to watch people develop insight into their behaviours and entertain possibility for change. I knew other General Practitioners who were able to wear both hats, i.e. do both physical medicine and psychotherapy, but not in the peaceful, calm way that was in the best interests of both the patient and the therapist. But once all my attempts at part-time psychotherapy had been sabotaged, I realized I would have to do it full-time or not at all. I knew many GPs who would happily refer their patients to me for psychotherapy because, as an MD, my services were fully covered by the provincial health plan. Also, many people only wanted to see a woman and others wanted to avoid the stigma of seeing a psychiatrist, so I was certain that my schedule would fill up quickly as a general practitioner practising only psychotherapy.

I was ambivalent about leaving my general medical practice behind. I knew I would miss certain individuals, the variety of problems, the fun entailed in seeing the kiddies and worst of all, I would no longer require a receptionist. I would have to give up my own personal psychotherapist, Larry. I worried I may not maintain a decent income. I wondered if the government would pull the plug and limit the amount of therapy one doctor could bill. I was concerned that leaving my physical medicine skills behind meant that in the future I would never be able to retrieve them.

On the other hand, giving up physical medicine would mean I could once again have painted fingernails.

After much difficult deliberation I put my general practice up for sale. I wasn't selling my patients. I was attaching a price to the goodwill involved in passing along a functioning office in downtown Toronto, with detailed files on people to whom I would recommend the replacement doctor. As there was no doctor shortage in the '80s as there is now, the only way for a new graduate to be busy immediately was to take over a large pre-existing office. My practice, however, was unusual in that I saw only one patient every 15 minutes, which meant I only managed to see 28 or 30 people a day, a decent income, but insufficient for most eager recent grads—especially males—who wanted to see up to 60 patients per day.

The sale took eighteen months of advertising, networking and interviewing before I finally met with a middle-aged GP who had a family in Grand Bend and wanted to come out of the closet into gay-town Toronto. What attracted him to my practice was the location near Church and Wellesley and the fact that Larry agreed to stay on as receptionist.

As Larry so wisely taught, we celebrated every step of the way: first, when the verbal agreement was made, then when we signed the papers and a third time when the new doctor actually began seeing my patients in July of 1986. I was finally free to pursue full-time psychotherapy.

After the sale, inquiries continued to come in from potential buyers, so I passed on the names to Jonathan. Despite reservations about insufficient income from full-time psychotherapy, he decided to sell his general practice to a family doctor from Ottawa, thereby making the identical change in scope of practice as I had.

Jon and I decided to take a trip before becoming full-time 'GP Psychotherapists', or 'GPPs'. Before leaving Toronto, I had a few months to wait and needed cash for the trip. I approached a group of women family doctors down the hall from my former office on Church Street and asked about using their office for a short time before our trip abroad to see a few new psychotherapy patients. I wanted to be as busy as possible and they were delighted to refer patients to me. I agreed to see all who called.

My first patient was referred by her family doctor who told me the woman only required regular supportive psychotherapy. Kristine was a pleasant woman with long black hair, bright red lips and thick features. She arrived in my temporary office carrying a square white plastic purse.

"Oh, Dr Baltman, I'm so glad I got to see you," she said in a husky tone. "After many drawn-out tortured years, I finally got my surgery. For ten years I did the hormones, but the clinic at the Clarke kept refusing the surgery. They never told me why. For years, I worked my day job as a woman. I didn't just get dressed up in the evenings to party, like the trannies. I lived my entire life as a woman. Can you imagine how awful that was to get refused year after year?" she continued telling her story without a single question from me.

"But now I am a full-fledged woman. Aren't I gorgeous? I am so proud."

"So why are you coming to see me now?" I asked.

"Well, I was sexually abused as a kid by my babysitters, both male and female. My uncle also abused me. It's always been tough for me. But I got through it all. Until now... One year after my surgery, I met the love of my life. A beautiful, gentle man waltzed into my arms. It was so wonderful. We fell madly in love. He was unemployed, but that didn't matter. We could live on love. I worked days at Shoppers as a cashier and did nights waitressing at the Winchester. We quickly moved into a rooming house together, down the street from work. I supported him and his cigarettes. I didn't care that he sat at home all day and smoked. For the first time in my life, I was content. Things were great. And then, there was the fire," she said, her eyes sinking in, her body slumping.

"I came home that Saturday night, with my pockets loaded with tips from a really busy shift. I was excited to tell Sam all about it. Then I saw the police cars and fire trucks. Tons of them. Outside our house. The fire was out. It stank. Some drunk told me that someone died in the fire. I told a cop I needed to go in and get my stuff. That I lived there and my boyfriend was inside.

"'You can't go in there. It's not safe,' the cop barked at me. I told him my boyfriend was in there and I started shouting that I had to find Sam.

"'There's no one in there alive,' he said. 'They found one body on the third floor. Someone fell asleep smoking on the couch. They burned down the whole building. Dead dog, too....' The damned cop kept yammering at me. I didn't really hear him. I was spaced out.

"'Who died?' I screamed at that idiot. 'Was it Sam?'

"'Don't know, lady. Go to Wellesley emerg, maybe they'll tell you there,' the useless cop said.

"'I have to go in and see my place!' I demanded.

"'Off limits. Go to the hospital. Or read about it in the paper in the morning.' He tried to slough me off. I was about to push past him, when his buddy moved in. I just kept screamin' at the both of them.

"'I need to find Sam! I need to find Sam!' I kept saying. And it *was* Sam. And my five-year-old dog, Sue. All gone. In one night. I was finally happy and then his damned cigarettes did us in. I didn't mind payin' for them, but did he have to go and burn the whole bloody house down? My life was over. Right then. No point."

Silence…

"So I've come to talk about dealing with my depression until the anniversary of the fire next month, 'cuz that's when I'm gonna kill myself. I can't go on living. I have to get back to Sam. I saved up the pills they gave me for depression. I'll take them all, get into the bathtub and just fade away. And don't you try to give me anti-depressants. I won't take them. I'll save them up. This is my plan and you can't talk me out of it. It makes perfect sense. I feel totally fine about it. Except for my mother. She'll be really upset, although we never got along anyway. Even when I was really little, she got upset with me when I wanted to dress as a girl. Never did see eye to eye. There's no way I can please her now."

"Look, I'd really like to help you and listen to your problems," I said.

"Great, so I'll come back next week at the same time?" she asked, lifting her head and looking straight at me.

"First I have to get some input from a more experienced physician about your plans to kill yourself."

"No way," she said. "I have a plan and no one is going to stop me."

"I won't stop you, but we need to help you find alternatives. This is not your only option. We could get help from a specialist to see what we could do together, but I don't want to force an assessment against your will," I said, beads of sweat multiplying on my forehead. "You've worked hard to get your surgery. You are finally the physical person you've always wanted to be. I'm sure we could help you emotionally in some way so you can carry on with your life."

Kristine paused… "Look, I know I've laid a lot of shit on you in my first visit. I really have no intention of doing anything 'til our anniversary date a month from now. I only need someone to talk to over the next month. I can talk to you pretty easily. Can't I just come back here and talk? That's all I want."

"Okay. Why don't we meet soon to talk things over," I agreed, my heart racing. "But you have to promise not to do anything to hurt yourself before seeing me again."

"I already told you I won't do anything until the anniversary date."

We agreed on an evening appointment two days later. She left the office. I was shaking. My first psychotherapy patient was acutely suicidal. Alternatives to her plan would only become clear to her with treatment, but I had no idea how to get her that treatment. She was willing to come back to my office, but unwilling to see anyone else.

I was scared and needed help to handle the situation. I called several psychiatrist colleagues, including Rowena, who made practical suggestions. First of all, Kristine needed to see a psychiatrist to determine if she required hospitalization with constant monitoring to protect her from herself. If she refused that consultation voluntarily, I would have to fill out a legal document called a Form One declaring that the patient was at risk to themselves or others and required psychiatric assessment in hospital. If she refused to comply with the Form One, the police would have to be called to take her against her will. This was all new terrain for me and I was terrified what her response might be.

Kristine's next appointment was in the evening when I would be alone with her in the office and feared she could totally freak out that I was interfering with her scheme. I was secretly hoping my problem would go away by her not showing up, as I had no address or phone number to find her. My first patient after the change of focus in my practice was overwhelming, but I had no choice, I had to proceed.

The evening of her appointment arrived and I was nervous. She showed up, poised and calm. I called her into the consulting room. "I've thought a lot about what you told me on your last visit. The fire was a horribly devastating event for you."

"That's the understatement of the half century!" Kristine laughed.

"I can understand how you are feeling. You've experienced a huge loss, causing you tremendous grief and pain, which could make you feel that the only way out is to end your life. But there *are* alternatives. Right now it's difficult for you to see them in your state."

"I'm not in a state. I'm perfectly level-headed."

"You're right. You are level-headed right now. But what about if we got you into a safe place for the time around the anniversary? Somewhere you won't have to worry about a roof over your head or what food to eat? Somewhere you'll have people to talk to all the time? You'll get a break to think otherwise about your plan. It would be somewhere that you won't be able to hurt yourself. Just give it a try," I pleaded.

"I don't know what good it'll do. I don't want my life."

"Just think about the possibility," I said. "I can get a colleague-friend to see you. He's a psychiatrist. He's a pretty understanding kind of guy."

"Ya, right. I bet he is."

"How about it? We'll get you to the hospital, just for the assessment."

"Well, maybe for the assessment. But I'm warning you, if they admit me and I want outta there, I'll bust my way out if I have to."

"Fine, just give it a try," I replied.

Kristine agreed and I called St Mike's emerg, where I had already arranged a consultation for her with a staff psychiatrist and told them she was coming. Then I called a taxi. Kristine sat in my waiting room until the cab arrived.

An hour later, the phone rang. It was the resident in psychiatry who saw Kristine in emerg before the staff man got there: "You're just sloughing her off," he rudely announced. "You could have continued to see her in your own office but you're going on sabbatical out of the country, so you want us to admit her to take her off your hands."

"Excuse me?" I choked, barely able to speak to the resident who'd already hung up on me. *So what did that mean? That if I wasn't going away, I could easily handle this sexually abused, trans-*

gendered, suicidal woman in my office? That otherwise she wouldn't need psychiatric assessment?

Kristine sounded more logical to me than this resident. He sounded exactly like the one I'd run into in the early days of my practice with Mrs Justen, my ninety-three-year-old patient with pneumonia.

Later that day I heard from the staff psychiatrist that Kristine had been admitted. Several weeks later, he called again to explain that Kristine had remained in hospital over the time of her anniversary and she had agreed to take antidepressants. She had even allowed her mother to visit and they had reconciled. She was feeling much better, was no longer suicidal and was about to be discharged to be seen regularly in follow-up in the out-patient clinic.

What I learned from discussing this woman with Rowena and others was the importance of initial triage, or sorting of patients. As a GP practising psychotherapy, I had been seeing only people with whom I was already well-acquainted. But when taking unknown referrals from other GPs, I would have to carefully screen those I agreed to help and also cautiously choose those to whom I turned for help. Being a solo health care provider without a surrounding team to handle people with complicated needs, I could only book patients for assessment if they fulfilled my criteria of requiring 'Primary Care Psychotherapy for the Walking Wounded'.

As a result, I began a rigid screening process. I returned patients' calls, then using a page from Dr Pindar's book about 'getting patients to chase you up a tree for treatment to achieve a more positive outcome', I placed them on a waiting list. I would call them back later, spending at least one-half hour on the phone with them. I would ask pertinent questions about their issues, trying to eliminate people with major mental health diagnoses or suicidal tendencies that would require greater expertise than I could provide.

Subsequently over the years, I devised additional techniques of triage, which were not infallible but helpful— not accepting relatives of existing patients, always getting a referral from the patient's GP, not taking on people because I thought I 'should', not taking patients who told me how wonderful they'd heard I was and that I'd be the only one who could help them. I learned to pay strict attention to alarm bells going off because those warnings were usually right. I spent my days teaching patients to trust their intuition so I needed to heed my own credo.

The few months before leaving on our trip provided me with a sharp learning curve in the practice of psychotherapy, which meant seeing fewer patients and therefore yielding less revenue than I had hoped for. I left Toronto with less money but with lovely long painted fingernails.

CHAPTER 15

A Bigger Switch

Before continuing with the huge change in our professional lives, we decided to take a break from Toronto and all medical employment. Jonathan and I hadn't travelled seriously since we journeyed around the world in 1972.

Our daughter Arielle was five. If we were to pull her out of school for a time, it would have to be before she started grade one. We debated where to go. I wanted to visit Senegal to be immersed in an exotic West African culture and the French language. Jonathan worried about our daughter's exposure to tropical health risks; he preferred a six-month sabbatical reading comfortably in our living room. After much debate, we reached a happy compromise, or so I thought. We agreed to travel to a far-off, yet safe British culture—New Zealand.

In October 1986, we arrived in Auckland with absolutely no plans. Spring was in the air, foliage bursting into bloom. With British culture, familiar language and friendly people, we thought it would be easy to settle in. First, we needed a car to get around the sprawling city. Then we had to learn to drive on the other side of the road. "Just follow the car in front of you," we were told, which worked until there was no one to follow, when it was easy to drift over onto the right side, or the wrong side. But slowly we learned.

Finding a house to rent for six months in our price range was an enormous task. A local real estate agent took us around to see one horrid dump after another. After much frustration, we found a great bungalow a bit out of town in Bucklands Beach, overlooking the harbour below. Once we settled into this quaint spot, all we had to do was water the endless waves of impatiens in the garden and keep the *spa*, or hot tub, functioning properly. When its motor went on the fritz, the owners' son amused us by saying he was *flummoxed* over being unable to fix it. His parents, our hospitable landlords, later offered us their *bach*, or cottage, on the South Island as well.

To my horror, I discovered that in 1986 there were no bagels in New Zealand and little else to feed my five-year-old who had been raised on them. She was already suffering from a short haircut from home, which made her look like a boy. And to make matters worse, she was neither blonde-haired and blue-eyed like the British kids, nor dark-haired and dark-skinned like the indigenous Maoris. Arielle's skin was white-white and her hair was brown-black, so her appearance *flummoxed* everyone there.

As we watched the sailboats drift in and out of the bay, the days flew by at Bucklands Beach. I enrolled in a course in feminist English literature at the University of Auckland and drove downtown to classes once a week from our suburban haunt. Soon it was Christmas and the *pohutukawa* trees were in bloom, looking like thousands of enormous red poinsettias hanging off the cliffs next to the tall golden grasses wafting in the warm breeze. Christmas in eighty-degree weather was delightful. The carollers came round to the house in shirt-sleeves and instead of shivering in the snow we stood there listening with the door wide open.

One week we drove up to the Coromandel peninsula and cooked clams freshly-picked from the beach across the street. We walked to the local fish stand and bought the catch of the day which the vendor told me how to cook. We even went to a rugby match starring the famous *All Blacks*.

Life was slower and all of New Zealand felt like Toronto in the '50s, yet in so many ways they were way ahead of us. Every kitchen had a microwave, every sink a garburator and every toilet flushed successfully.

Visitors soon began to arrive. Rowena, my Kiwi mentor extraordinaire from Toronto, was home visiting her family. She stopped by with her twelve-year-old daughter for an overnight before catching the plane back to Toronto. So we, the Torontonians, hosted Kiwis in Auckland. My mother and sister came to stay with us for a month to tour the North and South Islands. Mother Hellie practised her Tai Chi movements in green parks all around the country.

We learned to check for *huhus in our gummies*, bugs that snuck into our *wellies* overnight, which we had to dump out in the morning before going for a walk. In cool evening air we were told to put on a *cardie* before going out to cook steaks on the *barbie*. And we soon realized that we were the *pakehas* or foreigners in *Aotearoa*, a land steeped in the rich Maori culture.

Never once missing medical practice in Toronto, I suddenly found five months had passed and it was time to board the plane to visit Rarotonga in the Cook Islands en route home. We spent a glorious month in a small hotel on the beach overlooking the blue-green lagoon where we walked around clad only in bathing suits and *pareos* or sarongs and the locals made us bright pink frangipani *leis* from the gorgeous, ubiquitous blossoms. We watched Piri Piruto climb the tall coconut trees, throwing down the fruit that he later hacked open so we could taste its sweet milk and chewy pulp.

After skipping one entire Canadian winter, we flew home in May, returning to a beautifully renovated kitchen and main floor powder room, completed during our absence. As I had experienced after my round-the-world tour, returning home meant enormous culture shock. After six months of leisure, it was a whirlwind being back in fast-moving Toronto.

I wondered if it was worth doing all the work required to get away and then all the chores upon return in order to accommodate such big breaks away. Intellectually, I know it's essential—the benefits far outweigh the costs. But in the midst of the preparation beforehand or the recovery afterwards, it's difficult to see that pay-off.

What amazes me is that once I am away and pre-occupied with nothing but activities of daily sustenance, I can't imagine how my life gets so rushed and complicated when I'm working again. Even now in semi-retirement, my activities expand to fill my free days so I'm constantly in a hurry. Maybe in full-time retirement that mad dashing will go away? Some say it does, but I would bet that after a while, life takes over and the scurrying begins again. Unless, perhaps, one lives in New Zealand.

We settled into a dusty, post-renovation house and organized Arielle's summer schedule. I had six months of mail to catch up on. (Fortunately no email yet.) Family and friends were anxious to see us and psychotherapy patients were awaiting my return. I found a new office, a lovely place on Harbord Street on the second floor of an old Victorian building. My new landlady suggested another office for Jonathan to rent across town, which turned out to be perfect for his new psychotherapy practice. Life in Toronto resumed again and over the winter months our practices expanded.

The following spring Jon and I, my sister Lynni and her husband Brian were booked to fly to California for the weekend for her best friend's wedding. On the Thursday morning, I found a note from Jon on the kitchen counter that read:

I'm leaving. I'm not coming to California.

That was it. There was no reason, no discussion, no possibility for couple therapy for two psychotherapists. It was a total shock.

Somehow, I managed to choke down some breakfast, crying. A full day of patients ahead, I had to pull myself together to get to the office to focus on the problems of others.

The next day, I flew off to California with my sister and brother-in-law as planned, struggling to process what had happened. I had not seen the break-up coming. I was devastated.

Jon and I had a long history together, including lots of fun. I thought our values coincided. The relationship was not perfect but we were great co-parents and excellent business partners. For me, the hardest part of the split was facing the fact that the person I had considered my closest friend and ally suddenly turned hostile and combative.

The first year was brutal dealing with Jonathan's re-marriage. Suddenly having my daughter with me only half-time, I grew out of touch with her activities from one-half of her week and from the alternate weekend. I missed her. Her life carried on as before, only she had to contend with two houses, two rooms, two sets of clothes and rules and a new step-parent. My heart ached for her. I tried to be both mother and father to her when she was with me, which was exhausting and unrealistic. She tried to take care of me by not telling me fun or exciting details about what went on over there, lest I felt badly about missing it. To protect me from the full financial weight of her expenses, she went to his house even when she didn't want to. I tried to let her know she didn't have to look after me but she persisted. Jon bought her expensive clothes and sneakers, yet at the tender age of seven she understood that I had to be cautious with my spending, so she didn't demand designer clothes like other kids did. Gradually, we developed our new routine.

My career carried on as before. I found that being single in my early forties was an enormous opportunity for growth and experience. For the first time in years, I had time for myself, hours, evenings, even days when I could just relax on my own and function at a slower pace. I was cancer-free and aside from chronic migraines, my health was good. I went dancing with girlfriends and took some courses.

What had started out as a switch in the scope of my professional practice turned out to entail radical changes in every aspect of my life. Within two years, I had a new office, new practice, new house and had become a single parent. I managed to survive it all, as we humans somehow come upon astonishing strength in times of crisis. When my lease on Harbord Street ended, I knew I was ready to take on yet another challenge.

CHAPTER 16

Israel

From an early age, my connection to Israel has always been visceral. After growing up in a conservative Jewish home, attending Hebrew Day School and a Labour Zionist camp as a teen, I finally travelled there while at university and loved it. I was in awe of a people ready to commit their children to defending a land they believed was rightfully theirs, and impressed by their determination to carry on in spite of attacks and explosions. I enjoyed the spirit of the place, the spontaneity, the intensity of every moment. Although we had many opportunities throughout married life to attend medical conferences there, Jonathan feared the violence, so we never went to Israel. Perhaps I wanted us to enjoy vacations as a couple, be the good wife and not rock the boat, though I still can't fully understand why I didn't go on my own.

I was standing in the shower one day when suddenly the old yearning came back. It was early 1991 in my new home after the divorce. I fantasized about doing volunteer work on a kibbutz and as Arielle, at age ten, was attending Hebrew Day School in Toronto, she would be well-equipped to manage at school in Hebrew. Being away from the rigours of a Toronto schedule, she and I would get more quality time together or so I imagined.

1991 was an exceptionally optimistic time in Israel. Things were relatively calm. The peace process was beginning, which led to the Oslo Accord signed by Bill Clinton, Yasser Arafat and Yitzchak Rabin on the White House lawn, winning them the Nobel Peace Prize in 1994. Everyone hoped the days of teenage army recruits being killed defending their homeland would be over, freeing them up to pursue more Western ideals of drugs and rock 'n' roll. Buoyant years which would abruptly grind to a halt in 1995 with Rabin's assassination.

I wrote to the Israel Medical Association which connected me with Dr Chiskin, a family physician, who eventually found us room and board on a kibbutz in the Galilee in exchange for my volunteer services as a GP psychotherapist. It took months to finally settle on a tenant for my house and someone to take over my practice. I spent a year discussing my impending departure with patients who were excited for me but understandably apprehensive about their care. Week after week, we probed intensely into their feelings of loss and abandonment.

After working as a psychotherapist for four years, my physical medicine tools were a bit rusty. I hadn't worked in an emergency department for fourteen years so my trauma talents were dusty. Facing a country with a history of unrest, I wanted to feel more secure in my life-saving skills, so although I had previously trained in Basic Cardiac Life Support (BCLS), before leaving I also took an Advanced course (ACLS) at George Brown College.

Arielle's father was not happy about her going to Israel, despite the opportunity for an exceptional learning experience, saying it would disrupt her school and home-life. He would miss her and she would miss her friends and family. At that time, Family Law in Ontario was becoming quite stringent regarding anyone with joint-custody taking a child out of the country without written approval from the other parent. So my biggest concern was getting consent for her to leave Canada with me for a year. The back-and-forth communications began. Only when I consented to cover all of Arielle's expenses for the entire year, including weekly phone calls and a trip home for Christmas, did Jonathan agree to provide the requisite notarized letter.

Over the months of planning, several options fell through, causing me to doubt the feasibility of my proposal, but then alternatives arose and I pressed on. By July, the details were arranged and I faced an enormous flurry of activity.

In August of 1992 we flew to Tel Aviv. The head of the volunteer association was due to meet us at the airport, but after an hour's wait, during which the entire airport emptied, we took a cab downtown to the Ami Hotel.

Welcome to Israel...

Exhausted from our 13-hour flight, we emerged from the taxi and walked up to the front desk with our bulging suitcases. We got our key and were directed to the elevator, which was too small for more than one person and one bag. I squeezed in as Arielle plunked down on the only item in the bare lobby—a grotty old sofa.

"Wait here, I'll be right back," I said, hitting the button for the fourth floor. I pushed my luggage out and down the hall and unlocked the door. The tiny, spartan room revealed two narrow single beds attached to opposite walls. A torn beige curtain fluttered over the barely-covered window. A sliding door opened onto a narrow cubicle with a sink and a toilet, which had a shower head over it. I crammed my valise between the two beds and trundled downstairs to request a larger room.

"No," he said.

"There is no bigger room in the whole hotel?" I asked.

"No." I had pre-paid one night so I wasn't about to pay for a second room at another hotel. We had no choice. Arielle picked up her bag and we jammed ourselves into the elevator. There was no need to describe the room to her—she knew exactly what it was like from the look on my face when I came downstairs. We piled our cases one on top of the other in the middle of the room, washed our faces and wandered outside to find breakfast or lunch, because we weren't sure which we needed or what time it was. We were about to stay in the first of many in our travels that would come to be known as 'prostitute hotels'.

The next morning, I called Dr Chiskin who cheerfully told us to catch a bus from the old central Tel Aviv station to Chadera and she promised not to stand us up like her colleague had done the night before. Stepping into the damp heat of the Chadera bus station, we were surrounded by people scurrying in all directions. Fumes from departing buses thickened the heat. Newspaper vendors called out headlines in unfamiliar cadences. Middle-Eastern tunes whined from the music shop and the smell of fresh chocolate wafted from the Elite candy store. Arielle flopped down listlessly on our bags.

Roaming around the bus station searching for a woman I didn't know, I wondered: *Where have I dragged my sweet Arielle? Into this thick August heat of Israel—just like the dense Ghanaian temperatures. But at least we'll be in the north where it's cooler, not in the southern desert...* I looked up to see a white Subaru slamming up to the curb. A slim, blonde, middle-aged woman jumped out and came straight towards us.

"Sharon, Arielle, welcome. Give me your bags. Let's go," she instructed in perfect English. In a second, Dr Chiskin tossed a year's worth of baggage into her tiny trunk, we hopped in and were off. Thankfully, the air-conditioning was on full blast. Darting her car through heavy traffic, she told us to call her Zahava, saying she would drive us directly to our apartment on Kibbutz B'Seder.

Stopping the car on a deserted sandy parking lot next to rows of identical two-storey austere buildings, she hopped out and quickly led us up a flight of terrazzo steps to our 'room'. We stepped into an open salon with mini-fridge, hot plate, bathroom and a few basic furnishings. There was a tiny bedroom for me and a smaller one for Arielle, fitting only a single bed and a desk. Zahava switched on the clunky old air-conditioner and closed the windows and shutters to keep out the hot air, making the room feel like a dungeon. She explained that she was the head of the family practice department at the nearby Chadera hospital and would pick me up for rounds the next morning at the kibbutz gate at 8. She left as quickly as she had appeared.

Arielle and I looked around the room, then at each other, both realizing at that moment that we were stranded in the middle of nowhere, not knowing a soul, without food or linens. "I guess this is home," I attempted, trying to hide my tears. "Let's unpack and wash up. Maybe that'll make us feel better."

I barely had time to process how displaced I was feeling when the phone rang. It was Arielle's future classmates, curious to check out the alien intruder from 'Amerika'. They soon arrived en masse, gabbing away rapidly in teenage idiomatic Hebrew which I couldn't understand but Arielle did, and then left.

A few minutes later, our downstairs neighbour called to welcome us, explaining that everyone who came to live on the kibbutz was 'adopted' by a local host family who would introduce them to the community and provide a home base. She told us that our assigned 'adoptive' family was currently away from the kibbutz, so in their stead she was inviting us down to visit.

Suri was seventy-three years old and had moved from Romania in the late 1930s to be one of the original members of the kibbutz. She had lived her entire life there with her children and grandchildren. She arranged linens and offered to take us to the *super* (market) to buy food staples. She taught us to find our room amid the cluster of apartments that all looked the same by the smell of the *refet* (barn) across the road, so we'd know we were home. She entertained us with stories about the kibbutz and later became our surrogate mom and grandmother.

Not only did Arielle have to start school the next day, it was also her eleventh birthday. I had no cake, no present and no family or friends to greet her. When she returned to our bleak apartment after school she refused to give any details about her day. We had nothing else to discuss and not even a TV to watch. We sat there fidgeting, tense and silent, waiting for Gila, an Israeli relative of a Canadian friend, who had promised to take us out for dinner and go to a mall to buy Arielle a present. Then the phone rang. My older sister, Rena, was calling from Toronto to wish Arielle a happy birthday. I passed the phone to Arielle, who had no idea why I was crying.

I felt overwhelmed, disappointed and exhausted. After all the months of preparation, re-organizing and packing, we had finally reached our destination—a tiny stark room on an enormous farm smelling of cow-shit. We had no choice. We had to make the best of it, as my mother used to say. I told Arielle we would have to take it one day at a time, try to laugh when we could, cry when we couldn't laugh and hope that slowly, kibbutz activities would distract us.

The kibbutz in Israel began as a collective settlement of individuals living together, where—'Each shall contribute according to his ability and receive equally'—a socialist part of the Zionist ideal that developed in Europe in the late 19th Century. After Israel was declared a state by the United Nations in 1948 as a homeland for Jews after the devastation of World War II in Europe, many kibbutzim sprouted all over Israel in order to re-populate and cultivate the countryside. City populations expanded simultaneously with a Western lifestyle totally different from the kibbutz. The early kibbutzim, with two to fifteen hundred inhabitants, boasted common dining areas, laundries and children's houses where kids played, ate, learned and slept together. The grade six group of kids who came to greet Arielle had lived together since birth like brothers and sisters in such a children's house. Parents lived elsewhere, early on in tents and later in humble rooms like the one we had. Members worked diligently together to contribute to the growth of the kibbutz, many of which became successful in a variety of areas such as agriculture, factory production, exporting and fishing. However, with people spending so much time together like one giant family, competitions and jealousies inevitably arose, with gossip and petty disputes erupting.

Over the years, communal living got diluted as members wanted to work off the kibbutz, keep their own salaries, buy their own cars and become more materialistic just like in the city. By the time we arrived, things had evolved dramatically and the children were now living with their parents in larger, renovated homes. Only communal dining, laundry and schooling continued.

Things changed even more after we left, when people began taking meals in their own rooms. Today *kibbutznikim* (kibbutz members) are more individualistic. Most work off the kibbutz, the dining room is closed and most kibbutzim resemble villages of independent families. The old Socialism gradually faded into Capitalism. The lifestyle Arielle and I lived that year is all but gone.

Though I had been assured of work, I didn't know ahead of time that Kibbutz B'Seder already had a GP and a social worker, so it turned out that my medical services were not needed. In order to live on the kibbutz and have Arielle go to school there, I was required to contribute work-wise. I investigated a job as assistant to the woman-in-charge of the old folks' home, but she was an obstinate lay person and when she heard I was an MD declined working with me.

Another work placement offered was as nurse-maid to a forty-year-old man who had apparently crashed a kibbutz car while speeding and ended up blind with multiple disabling injuries. In the interview, all he wanted to know was how I felt about helping him naked into the shower. I refused the job.

The only remaining work option available to me was in set-up and clean-up of the *chadar ochel* (dining room). For the next month, I got up at 5 am, trekked all the way to the dining hall, wiped down tables and filled salt and pepper shakers and oil and lemon juice bottles. Every morning I put out breakfast buckets of hot cereal, cold cereal, *laban* (liquid yogurt), tomatoes and cucumbers. I filled metal trays with olives and pickles made by our kibbutz. I loaded lunch carts with *tabouli* salad, mashed potatoes and fried fish. After meals, I cleaned tables, emptied yogurt containers, put away the 16-slice toaster and hosed off the food carts. My hands were raw, my fingernails cracked and broken. I was feeling beholden to others for making the kibbutz opportunity available to me and unfamiliar with local rules, felt I needed to tow the line and do as told, but as a result I ended up feeling infantilized.

After every meal, when big buckets of hot water and squeegee sticks with *smartoots* (rags) on the ends appeared, I would quietly disappear into the bathroom and hide for twenty minutes while the water was dumped out, the mops scraped the grease off the floor and it was all wiped back up. Then I'd casually emerge, mingling at the edge of the group, until they all dispersed to their respective rooms. At 45, I decided not to risk destroying my back for the remainder of my working career.

My professional skills were being ignored. When word got around that I was a psychotherapist, several women approached me saying they could fill my entire calendar with appointments for other English-speakers on the kibbutz. I decided it was time to end my demeaning experience in the *chadar ochel*. I booked an appointment to meet with the secretary of the kibbutz (CEO), a tall, handsome woman I hadn't met yet from one of the prominent families. Warned by savvy *kibbutznikim* to plead my case in a gentle, obsequious way, I walked nervously into her office and told her I had been unable to find suitable work within the kibbutz. Instead, I offered to pay a sum of cash per month for room and board for myself and my daughter so I could volunteer my professional skills at the local hospital. She was very understanding, agreed to a reasonable amount and we had a wonderful chat about a variety of topics. I was delighted.

Throughout the early months, Zahava, the blonde dynamo, continued to come and collect me at the gate to take me into

Chadera on my days off. She insisted I go to lectures and teaching sessions with her that were mostly in Hebrew. The only words I had trouble understanding were names of diseases and body parts, which were not taught in primary Hebrew day school. So I bought a three-ring binder and began recording unfamiliar words, looking them up later in the evening on my *Targumon*, a primitive electronic dictionary that was a very modern gizmo at the time. I typed a word in English or Hebrew characters on the keyboard of the 8×11 inch thick black plastic pad, hit enter and the meaning appeared on a small screen in the top right-hand corner.

Zahava introduced me to all the medical staff in the region and asked me to do some teaching in psycho-social issues. One week, I prepared a lecture in English on the topic of 'transference', the psychoanalytic term meaning redirection of a patient's feelings for a significant person onto the therapist and 'counter-transference', redirection of a therapist's feelings toward a patient. I arrived early for the teaching session and found no one there. Already nervous, I doubted that I was in the right place. As my Israeli colleagues trickled in, they reassured me it was okay to arrive late for lectures in Israel, but one must always arrive early if food is involved. The discussion afterwards was in Hebrew, but we all managed, as they had studied from English textbooks in medical school.

I noticed that an essential topic for healers in that country was care of the caregivers. Doctors were often dealing with trauma and death in healthy young people because of war injuries and suicide bombings which intensely affected them emotionally. There was no support system for healers and I worked on finding some method to help, but there was no money for it. Doctors' support was not covered by *Kupat Cholim*, the Israeli public health insurance system and was too expensive to be paid for out of their own pockets. Time was also an issue—the doctors were too busy in their own practices to care for themselves. After I left, doctors in the nearby city of Haifa were still working on the project.

Now that my dining room duties were over, Zahava encouraged local family doctors to refer patients to me for psychotherapy and I began a new schedule of travelling by public bus one day a week to each of three different clinics in Afula Ilit, Nazareth Ilit and Beit She'an. The moment I walked through the front door of the jammed clinics, aides jumped up to serve me hot sweet Moroccan *thé nana* (mint tea).

One day I spoke to a religious woman from Beit She'an, a primitive community from Morocco. She was abused by her traditional husband and forced to stay home even though they needed income to support an older, isolated relative who didn't speak the language.

Another day I saw a recent Russian immigrant who was eager to talk to someone about her problems with conditions in Israel, but she couldn't speak Hebrew yet. We couldn't communicate in Russian, so she spoke to me in Yiddish, which to my astonishment I understood and I responded using high school German. A professional violinist back home, she had emigrated to seek a better life, but instead ended up living in a scrawny integration trailer, studying Hebrew. Because I didn't charge for my services, many patients didn't show up, so I had time to sit and hand-write letters home, excitedly detailing my adventures to my mother, including how I understood Yiddish far better than I thought.

One of the social workers from Beit She'an took me along with her to Malkishua, a drug rehabilitation centre, established in 1990 high in the Gilboa Mountains. There we met young men who had emerged from the army with drug addictions and Post Traumatic Stress Disorder. In the wars they had witnessed horrific scenes of rapes and killings and did drugs to try to forget what they had seen. The centre also treated civilian men, women and youth with addictions and recently set up a separate section to treat only orthodox patients.

Zahava suggested I write articles from a Canadian perspective on the many conferences I attended and she arranged for publication either in Hebrew or English. She ensured I got paid for the articles and all the teaching I did. She invited Arielle and me to all her department dinners and offered us a tour of new housing developments. *Sabra*, a word referring to a native Israeli, is also a local fruit which is prickly on the outside and soft and mooshy on the inside. The term suited Zahava perfectly. She was brisk and brusque in her actions, yet funny, warm and helpful; she was efficient, independent and very smart. She was also totally devoted to her family, particularly to her husband who was a lot older than she. Zahava was loved by patients and respected by colleagues.

For the first three months, Arielle and I struggled in parallel, sharing our troubles and possible solutions. At times I thought we would never make it through the year though we never discussed returning home. While I was sorting through my work peregrinations, Arielle was going through her own traumas: a girl in her class was bullying her; math and geography in Hebrew were gruelling; she longed for home. Our assigned adoptive family, originally from Canada, returned and tried to help us out. Instead of asking Arielle how her day went, Rachel, our adoptive mom, wisely learned to ask her what had gone wrong that day, thus enabling Arielle to discuss her woes. Arielle was strong-minded and independent, determined to work things out her own way (like her mother!).

As her Christmas trip home approached, I feared she would never come back. We drove to the airport in silence. My tears eliciting only her disdain, she boarded the plane with the assigned cabin staff at 2 am. I drove off to meet Karen, the Canadian cousin of a Toronto friend, who, thirty-five years earlier had married an Israeli and settled on a kibbutz near the airport. Now divorced, she had spent her entire adult life on the kibbutz. She met me at the gate to let me in and although we'd never met before, we sat up talking and giggling until 5 am. Such was the nature of connection in Israel. We spent a couple of days together, touring her kibbutz and meeting people she'd known forever. She still kept in touch with dear old friends in Winnipeg who sometimes sent her money for a ticket home.

Although it was a bit chilly in December, I decided to treat myself to a weekend on my own in the southern resort town of Eilat. It was a relief to be away from the oppressiveness of the kibbutz, seeing the same faces every day and having my every action monitored. I missed my family and friends, the independence of my own home and car and the art and culture of the big city. But wandering around Eilat, I enjoyed every minute of time spent by myself.

Returning to the kibbutz, I resumed my activities. The first evening, I went dancing with the young folks at *Publool*, the disco located in a former chicken coop. The next night, I shared a 'Mac 'N' Cheese' dinner with a couple from Toronto who had made *aliyah*, intending to stay in Israel forever. Later that week, an American-born, Israeli-bred single mom took me to a singles dance off the kibbutz. One entire afternoon I spent downstairs visiting with Suri deep in discussion in Hebrew about politics and the future of Israel. The following week-end I attended a communications workshop in Tel Aviv, where I met Vicki, a physiotherapist and her family doctor-husband, Sasson, who invited us to visit them on their kibbutz by the ocean. I loved conversing with some people in English, others in Hebrew and some in *Heblish*, a mixture of both. I suddenly realized that in these few months I had established quite a social life.

During my free time in Israel, I had planned to catch up on my medical reading. In one of the magazines dragged with me, I found a creative writing contest with the prize of a computer, a very exciting prospect in 1992. I didn't even know how to turn one on. Back in Toronto, many times I had considered taking computer courses but couldn't fit one into my schedule. I decided to enter the competition with a piece about our adventures in Israel, but my illegible hand-writing was a problem. Rachel, our adoptive mom, offered to lend me her old manual typewriter sidelined by her first computer, a recent essential in every kibbutz household.

I bashed away on the typewriter, completed my article and with as few white-out corrections as possible, submitted it. It was published, but didn't win the contest. I was inspired to write more, and seeing Israeli children's facility with computers, and feeling like the Canadian Luddite, I was determined to use an electronic keyboard. I spent torturous hours in the cramped computer room on the kibbutz, at first writing step-by-step instructions how to turn it on, open a program, create a file, save, then print. All commands were via function keys as there was no mouse. I returned Rachel's clunker and began to mail home copies of legible group letters. It is almost impossible now to imagine not being familiar with what is today so automatic.

For outings on my own, I rented a kibbutz car. One evening I drove to another kibbutz near the Jordanian border to visit a colleague. The next day, *kibbutznikim* were astonished to hear that I had driven that far alone at night. Another night, driving to a singles party, I had trouble keeping up with my friend's car. I drove faster and faster and only when the car behind me began flashing their lights like a police car did I slow down and stop. In fact it was my friends, who had ended up behind me, informing me that I was on the wrong road heading into the Arab-Israeli town of Tulkarm. In those days it was possible to drive almost anywhere and I felt safe and confident doing so.

As the days flew by, I got nervous that Arielle wouldn't return. But there she was, patiently waiting for me at the airport as planned. I was overjoyed. She boldly declared she hated Toronto and preferred to 'go into the army, have babies and stay in Israel forever'. I was stunned. I had no idea what caused her sudden change of heart. But her extreme statement made me realize that in spite of all our difficulties at the outset, the country had seeped into our beings. I, too, could imagine myself staying forever.

The visceral attachment I had developed to Israel as a young student returned. The excitement. The exuberance of the place. The importance and pertinence of every daily event all across the tiny country. The connection to everyone in one BIG community, with even fewer than six degrees of separation. The atmosphere was casual, with friends constantly dropping in. Friendships were instantaneous, enthusiastic and long-lasting.

For the first time in my life, I was not part of a minority, as everyone was celebrating the same holidays as I was. I loved the language and the expressiveness of it. And the ubiquity of sweets and chocolate enthralled me.

Not everything was perfect, of course. One surprise discovery was the *geezanut*, or racism, that existed: between Jews—with *Ashkenazim*, or Central and Eastern European Jews to include Americans at the top; then *Sephardim* or Spanish and Middle Eastern Jews; then Moroccans; then Russians; then black Ethiopians, derogatorily labelled *Kushim*; and then at the very bottom were Arab Israelis. I once watched as a white Israeli on a public bus refused to sit next to an Ethiopian. At school, darker-skinned Jewish children adopted from places like Central America were also called *Kushim*. And even though, while we were there, we were able to travel with caution to towns in the West Bank and Gaza to shop in the fruit markets, an awareness of the *other*, the 'Arab' population, was ever-present. It was still possible to drive the shorter route from the north of the country, through Nablus and Ramallah in the West Bank, right down to Jerusalem.

Palestinian workers still came and went across the borders into Israel from Gaza and the West Bank.

But later, after the wall was built, ostensibly to keep suicide bombers out of Israel, there emerged a gaping separation between Jewish Israelis and the *other*. Palestinians began waiting hours to pass through check-points in order to cross into Israel for work, supplies or hospital care. The longer route via Tel Aviv became the only way for Israelis to get from the north to Jerusalem, entirely avoiding what became the walled-off West Bank. Israelis could no longer shop where everyone had previously mingled peacefully together. Hierarchy was obvious when we were there, but after the wall, it became extreme. As a result, since we were there, some of my optimism about the country has soured.

Arielle's trip to Canada was a turning point. After coming back, she and I spent many wonderful, precious hours together. Most days after school we walked slowly up the hill to the swimming pool, found a spot in the shade away from the sticky heat and ate our picnic dinner of pitas filled with *chummus* or tuna and cucumber, with fruit and lots of chocolate wafer sandwich cookies. She entertained me by reading aloud her long English fiction compositions and doing funny imitations of her Hebrew teachers. She had the Israeli accent down perfectly and sounded exactly like a *Sabra* after only a few months in the country. She used Arabic expressions of *Yalla* (let's go) and *keff* (fun) like the local kids. We went on a hike together with *Haganat Ha'Teva*, the Society for the Protection of Nature, to get to know other areas of the country.

My mother came for a visit bringing us fresh stocks of Kraft dinner and a decent pillow for me. She stayed in the kibbutz guesthouse and we travelled with her to Jerusalem and Haifa. We later celebrated Arielle's almost reaching her Bat Mitzvah age of twelve with a service at the Western Wall and a dinner afterwards with our extended Israeli family. As difficult as it had been at the beginning, Arielle and I experienced more hours together than ever and had tons of *keff* (fun) and I learned again how to productively assert my own needs.

The kibbutz work had unravelled. I ended up paying for room and board, but Zahava was the machine that stitched it all together for us. The last I heard, she had worked her way through law school and is now representing patients in lawsuits against their doctors.

Why is it that rough times pass so slowly, yet good times, like the second half of our stay in Israel, fly by? I researched the possibility of remaining in Israel. *Kupat Cholim* would not pay for psychotherapy by a GP and there simply weren't enough people who could afford to pay for it privately. Family Medicine was one possibility that would have involved studying a lot more Hebrew than my binder full of words provided and it would have meant giving up the hugely important switch in my career to psychotherapy. Furthermore, Arielle needed to return to her family base with her father, cousins and grandmother. So the reality was that we could not stay forever. We had to pack our bags and cross the ocean again.

CHAPTER 17

Curve Balls

While I was away in Israel, my house on Hillsdale was rented out to a lawyer and his three sons, with a clause in the agreement stipulating that my regular cleaner would continue to go in every two weeks to keep the house in good shape.

On her first visit, she noticed a strange sewage smell. Thinking a drain had backed up, she checked the toilets and discovered all of them filled with excreta. She was told they were conserving water. From then on, as soon as she arrived she ran around flushing the toilets. She always found the kitchen floor covered with cereal spilling out of open boxes on the counter, next to four coffee machines constantly running and overflowing onto the floor. She refused to take off her coat, fearing the mice running around the kitchen would creep into her pockets.

Mounds of paper garbage filled the fireplace waiting to be burned and piles of compostable eggshells and bread crusts littered the front and rear garden beds, barely covered with earth. She witnessed his three sons, food in hand, sliding down the bannister, creating a sticky mess. Reluctantly, she continued to go in and mercifully never told me the details until I got home. What I did learn in Israel was that two months before the end of the lease, the tenant suddenly stopped paying rent and moved out.

Around the same time, a Canadian couple who had made *aliyah* (immigration to Israel) to our Kibbutz, changed their minds. They were returning to Toronto and needed a place to live. This unsuspecting couple and my cleaner had the enormous task of mopping up after the tenant-from-hell. They tried to spare me the worst, but could only restore the superficial. I arrived back to find large burns in the carpet in front of the fireplace. Melted wax had dripped from ledges and tables onto the floors of the bedrooms and bathrooms.

Blinds and shower curtains were yanked off their rods and left on the floor. Gashes on the walls next to the stairs from the basement marked the upward trek of the piano into the living room. Even a stash of porn flicks appeared in the cellar. When I signalled my intent to use the damage deposit to cover my repair costs, the tenant insisted he had only caused normal 'wear-and-tear' on the property. We compromised on an amount that covered little of the cost and time it took to rid the place of rodents and make the house liveable again.

In the fall of 1993, Arielle started back at Hebrew Day School in grade seven. Her old friends greeted her with curiosity about her year away. Her flowing musical Hebrew accent with guttural R's vanished as quickly as it had appeared, as she began to sound out Hebrew words phonetically in the North American way.

Needing an office to return to work, I rented space from two GP friends who sent me their well-screened patients for psychotherapy. I thought of how much easier it had been for Rowena, my supervisor, who worked from home, but couldn't imagine turning my dark cellar into an office.

"Why not?" my mother Hellie asked, when I mentioned the subject one day. "I see my podiatrist in his garage and your lower level is nicer than that. And he gets paid a lot more than you'll ever make from OHIP."

She was absolutely right. I always felt better after talking to Hellie. She knew how to deal with breast feeding problems, child-rearing issues, sleep difficulties, whatever I called her about. She knew how long chopped liver would keep in the fridge before going bad. No matter what the subject, my mother had great advice. She was self-taught through books and courses and travel and life in ways I could only aspire to. And truly she was always right.

So I listened to Hellie's wise words and called a couple of contractors for estimates, enlisted ideas from friends about how to transmit light from the back door through to what would become my consulting room. A lot of alterations had to be made.

As I stood there each morning, clipboard in hand, reviewing details with the contractor, he asked, "Have you been doing this for a long time?" Actually I had assiduously avoided renovations in the past to the point of going to New

Zealand while my kitchen on Lawton was completed so in fact I'd never done it before.

Three months later, the work was complete and I was ready to move into my new workspace. Arielle was excited to come home from school and have the entire house to herself knowing I was downstairs if she needed me. For the first time in her life, if she was ill she could stay home from school without major childcare chaos. I could care for her myself. She knew my schedule and was happy to wait until my lunch hour. At age twelve, she finally had a stay-at-home mom. Somehow this all began with our time together in Israel when she saw me more than she ever had and we bonded in a new way. We endured the traumas of travel together and though she may have grown up a little too quickly, she became a very wise soul.

The next summer, I opened the backyard swimming pool which had been neglected while I cleaned up from the tenant. When buying the house I thought of the pool as my consolation prize, a summer treat to replace my lost country property. It turned out that cleaning and testing the pool kept me so busy that I rarely had time to swim. But after magical pool parties, including a birthday celebration for Arielle, the house finally felt like my own again.

The new basement office functioned well and my psychotherapy practice was growing. One day after lunch, I went downstairs and stepping into my consult room, noticed something whip by me, disappearing under the pillow of my grey upholstered chair. I gingerly stepped closer to examine what looked like a tail sticking up from where I was due to be sitting talking to a patient, five minutes later.

Oh my God, what do I do? I wondered. *I have nowhere else to sit with my patient except in that chair.* I ran into the laundry room next door and rummaging in my toolbox, found a long pair of pliers, put on heavy winter work gloves, unlocked the back door to the pool and moved silently towards the tail, hands shaking. I grabbed it with my instrument and ran out the door, a mouse dangling at arm's length in front of me. Not wanting to drop it in the pool, I dashed to the far end of the yard and opened the pliers over the other side of the fence.

I walked slowly back into the house, trembling. To be sure there wasn't a family of them, I lifted all the cushions on my chair and on the patient's two-seater. I took a few deep breaths, patted cold water on my reddened face and tried to appear calm as I went out to bring in my next patient. During the entire session I kept seeing things flicking across my field of vision. The doctor was hallucinating... Obviously my tenant had left an enduring legacy.

One morning, a year later in 1995, after Arielle's friend Naomi slept over, we were all having breakfast in my freshly painted café-au-lait kitchen when Naomi asked, "What's that bump on your back?"

Arielle had been bending over the cutlery drawer and straightened up. "What bump?"

"No, bend over again," Naomi instructed. I set aside my bowl of raisin bran to inspect my daughter's back. She had a hump on one side of the back of her chest. To my physician eyes, it was obviously scoliosis, or curvature of the spine.

I asked my terrified fourteen-year-old all kinds of questions to which she had no answers: How long had it been there? Was it there in Israel? Did it hurt? When did she notice it? She hadn't noticed a thing. She had been to the paediatrician the previous year before sleepover camp and everything was fine. It was almost time to go again, as camp was starting in a month.

I took her to the paediatrician who confirmed the diagnosis and stated that it must be due to a rapid growth spurt. He referred her to an orthopaedic surgeon at the Hospital for Sick Children, but didn't know when she would get an appointment. A week later, when I hadn't heard from Sick Kids', I tried to use my influence as a physician to hurry up the process, but her doctor replied, "Sharon, I wish I could help you, but I have to save all my favours with the specialists for really sick children, like ones with suspected osteomyelitis, or bone tumours. I can't push for something like this, even if it's for the daughter of a colleague. That's just the way it is in medicine right now. I'm sorry. You'll have to wait until one of the offices calls you back with an appointment."

Our lives had suddenly changed. My nights were sleepless. My head was spinning with questions: *How could I have missed this obvious diagnosis? Especially after all the time we had spent together in Israel and during all this bonding while I was working at home? How did her doctor not see it last year at her check-up? If the curve had developed so fast, didn't it need to be assessed quickly before it worsened even more?*

I felt guilty. I felt stupid. I was worried. I was fitting the stereotype of a doctor healing others and not looking after her own. My daughter's rocky trip through adolescence, buffeted by hormones and moods, was becoming even more topsy-turvy.

Scoliosis is an abnormal curving of the vertebrae of the spine in the chest or lower back or both, which occurs in adolescence during periods of rapid growth. The cause is usually unknown. It often manifests as one shoulder or one hip being higher than the other, which is not often noticed until clothes become difficult to fit properly. At the time, treatments varied depending on the severity and the progression as measured by serial X-rays: from observation and doing nothing, to a brace or cast worn 24/7, to surgery with insertion of steel rods to stabilize the spine. If left untreated, the condition can result in severe deformity with painful arthritis in later years.

After what seemed like forever (probably only a few more days) I finally agreed to seek help from a family friend who got Arielle in to see a colleague who wasn't associated with the Hospital for Sick Children. A young, attractive orthopaedic surgeon, he was patient, kind and compassionate. "If she were my daughter, I'd put her in a body cast right away, 23 out of 24 hours a day and see how she progresses. You have nothing to lose."

Just after we got home from that appointment, Sick Kids' called with an immediate cancellation. We took her right back downtown to the orthopaedic surgeon there, who specialized in scoliosis and coldly stated, "The body cast won't do anything. From her X-rays, she is close to needing surgical stabilization. Do nothing and wait. If she gets worse, we'll operate and put in a rod."

It felt like a dagger in my heart. I was in tears, which I once again tried to conceal from Arielle. My heart was breaking for her. Where had this come from? We were just living our lives and suddenly this happened. Kibbutz problems were simple in comparison. My baby might have to have surgery and be forever impacted by a steel implant in her back. I knew a girl in high school who had one. She was flat on her back on a board for weeks. Afterwards, she had to learn to walk again. It was horrible. In addition, I had knowledge from my medical background that other moms didn't have—the awareness of possible complications of infection, of displacement of the rod, of endless time spent in hospital.

The decision lay with Jonathan and me. We were torn. At the awkward age of fourteen, a brace would be difficult for Arielle to manoeuvre, especially at camp. Yet we wanted to do whatever we could to avoid surgery. Even if the brace did no good, we would have tried. I had so many questions: *How could we ship her off to sleepover camp confined to a brand new body cast? For twenty-three hours a day? How would she sleep in a brace in front of all the other campers? Wouldn't she be too hot over the summer? How would she swim? How could she run and play baseball?* Even though she never swam and never played baseball. Keeping her home from camp was not an option, as she would be totally bored in the city because all her friends would be away.

Arielle wanted to wait and see. We decided to go for the cast. She was not happy with our decision, but agreed to co-operate. The brace needed to be fitted and made before she left for camp one week later. She had an appointment for the mould on Monday morning, the brace was ready on Thursday and on Saturday she got on the bus wearing it. I wept, she did not—at least not in front of me. It was made of poured plastic with leather wrapped around the edges and leather straps with Velcro closures. It went from under her breasts down to her pelvis to hold her spine as straight as possible. She could remove it only to shower and for one hour each day.

I worried about her every single minute, but there was nothing I could do. I had done all I could. Over the next few weeks, letters from camp were the usual *I-hate-it* routine. I tried to be empathetic about the brace.

"It's not the brace I hate, it's the kids," she wrote repeatedly. I guess this was just one more thing I didn't understand about teenagers...

But she did manage to survive the month. She came home and revealed no details about her ordeal or her feelings about it. All she said was that she had worn the brace as instructed. She was once again handling things her way. I flashed on this experience when recently, sixteen years later, there was a flood in her apartment and I offered to get involved and speak to her landlord and tell him what he should do. All these years later, she still has to tell me, "Mom, I can handle it myself."

Three months later, it was time for follow-up, but her orthopaedic surgeon had moved to the United States, so a resident saw us. She had her X-ray.

"Her back is improving, straightening," he said.

I was delighted.

"But wait... what's this?"

He was concerned about a large lymph node he noticed in her neck. He refused to listen to my protests that she had always been lumpy because she'd had recurrent ear and throat infections. I told him that in the past, I had felt that same nodule myself. He insisted on investigating her for cancer, with a biopsy and referral to an oncologist. I refused, leaving the office, agreeing only to follow-up with her own doctor.

The resident's new concern squashed my pleasure about her improved spine. With fresh anxiety, we raced around getting opinions from her paediatrician and then from a general surgeon, who deemed it a benign dermoid cyst, requiring removal for cosmetic purposes only. The irony being that once she entered the medical system, a totally benign discovery was singled out for immediate investigation. In the midst of dealing with one problem, we had gotten embroiled in a 'red herring', an unrelated but extremely daunting concern. One example of how an inexperienced but zealous physician can generate massive worry and cost. After facing the possibility of cancer, returning to the initial issue of scoliosis was a relief.

We continued with follow-up every three months. Her curve was decreasing, her back stabilizing. After one long year, to everyone's enormous relief, she could remove the brace. We kept it in a box in the basement for a long time as a reminder of what we had averted through the good advice of one young knowledgeable specialist.

The house on Hillsdale became the repository of a lot of history over a short period of time. At first I loved it and the office in the basement worked well for me. But the backyard pool was an annoyance, as I was constantly spending my week-end days buying chemicals, measuring pH, getting the heater fixed, cleaning leaves off the surface and serving drinks and snacks to endless summertime guests. Then the uninvited arrived: the raccoons. I spent my evenings chasing them from their nightly baths, even when the pool was covered for the winter. I ran around putting out hot pepper sauce, KY jelly and whatever else was suggested to scare the critters away. After several years of these shenanigans, the pool had become an enormous stone around my neck. In desperation, I contemplated filling it in.

Then other factors bothered me about Hillsdale. Craving to live further south, I wasn't at home in such a suburban-feeling area. Odd that there was such a difference between Yonge and Eglinton, versus Yonge and St Clair where I had lived comfortably on Lawton for years. I also longed to be free of the burden of home ownership that I had been carrying for twenty-five years. Real estate values were tumbling and a home no longer seemed such a good investment. Though I paid top market price for the house in 1989, interest rates were high and I thought I could cut my losses by investing my money elsewhere. Hoping to become a happy carefree tenant, I put my house up for sale. I dismissed Arielle's wise warnings that friends at school whose families rented moved frequently. I was determined.

After many months on the market, the house sold in 1997. I scurried around looking southward for an apartment to rent that would be suitable for home and office. Eventually I found a spacious, charming, two-storey unit in a huge, old renovated house on Biggar Avenue near St Clair and Oakwood. The move, which involved house and office simultaneously (I had never done that before), was difficult.

Arielle and I settled into the new place and it worked brilliantly both personally and professionally. But after only one year, our absentee landlord sold the house to a woman who moved in by kicking out the tenant from the main floor unit. The new landlady smoked in what was designated a non-smoking building. Though she was a nurse, she hassled my patients by running the sprinkler outside the front door during working hours and physically blocked access to my parking spot by standing in front of my car.

When we first moved in, a man was living in the basement apartment. He had been there for eight years and seemed a bit eccentric but I rarely saw him. After the building changed owners, he complained that things weren't the same. When he reported that the lock on his door wasn't working properly, nothing was done. He knocked on my door a couple of times late in the evening, apologizing profusely that he was locked out and needed access to his place through my unit. Some months later, his body was removed from the building. He had committed suicide. His death meant I was the only original tenant left.

Towards the end of my three-year-lease, the owner gave me notice to leave, saying that she was moving into my space (the only way a landlord in Toronto can legally throw someone out without reason). I appealed to the Landlord and Tenant Tribunal at City Hall and won the right to renew my lease for another two years, but the harassment had gotten to me. I was living with evil. For my own sanity I had to get out of there.

Eventually we moved to another very special two-storey apartment in an old house on Havelock Street at Bloor and Dufferin. I loved the area and the proximity to the shops on Bloor Street, but this time there were serious problems with noise coming from the tenants upstairs. With Arielle's wise observation—that renters move often—playing over and over in my head, my fantasies of ever being a happy tenant were gradually obliterated. After years of frustration, I concluded my efforts would be better channelled into a home of my own where I could make decisions for myself, without clomping above me or smokers below and asked my real estate agent to start looking.

CHAPTER 18

Loss

I first met Emma Silver in 1981. A recent medical graduate, she had moved to Toronto from Vancouver as I was searching for a locum for my maternity leave. The first thing I remember her saying was, "I don't have a car because that's too much like a grown-up", though by reputation she was indeed a very mature and smart doctor. From speaking with her I could tell she was extremely careful and conscientious, which would be great for my patients while I was away, but not for me later when I would be expected to devote similar attention to every minor detail. By comparison, I was less serious and more laissez-faire and needed my replacement to reflect my style. So I didn't hire her. Instead we became dear friends.

When I returned from mat leave, I offered her space to rent in my office on Church Street to start her own practice. She stayed late, often missing dinner, returned endless phone calls to anxious patients, made certain she reassured them about every query. When I suggested she might expend less energy caretaking and allow patients to accept more responsibility for their own health, she denied she was self-sacrificing, stating it was all part of the practice of good medicine. Some months later, she got busier and set up her own space with two other female GPs. At the time, she was living on her own, so I introduced her to my former office mate, Elvis Da Silva, who was also single. I warned him not to hurt my sensitive friend Emma.

Elvis was a tall, dark, good-looking man about my age whose warm handshake I'd noticed the first time Dr Goldglass introduced him to me in 1973. Our friendship had grown over lunches together at the office and intensified over dinners with our respective spouses. El was easy to talk to, warm, sincere and very charming. He was a huge support for me during my surgery and my father's death. When he left General Practice after his run at politics to do his psychiatry training, we continued to meet for collegial dinners several times a year. Emma and Elvis dated briefly. Later, he moved in with someone else but he and Emma continued a platonic relationship. Emma said she often remained friends with previous romantic interests.

Several years went by. When I moved into full-time psychotherapy, Elvis was a staff psychiatrist, so was very helpful around patient management. When my marriage dissolved, Elvis and I spent more time together and eventually became lovers. He was still living with his partner of more than five years. Claiming he feared massive emotional and financial fall-out, he insisted our relationship remain an absolute secret from everyone. I couldn't even tell my younger sister Lynni. Long before we got involved, he had confided his dalliances with other women so it was no surprise to me that he was not monogamous. I didn't have another man in my life when it started, but whenever I did, I ended the sexual part of my liaison with Elvis. As physicians cognizant of AIDS in the '80s and '90s, we both insisted upon safe sex. I was completely aware of what I was doing, or so I thought...

Through the years, Emma and I shared our clinical cases and had many heated intellectual debates. She was strong, rational, brilliant and on top of the latest medical literature. She looked up to me as a mentor, as the experienced, confident practitioner, yet I always learned from her. She taught me the importance of carrying a book or magazine at all times because you never know when you'll have to wait. If we were eating in a restaurant and I went to the bathroom, I often returned to find her deeply engrossed, underlining some article. She got involved in areas of medicine that I strongly believed in, but I could never devote the amount of energy that she did. She worked long hours on the Sexual Assault Team at Women's College Hospital, trying to change the medical process to avoid re-victimization of women. She impressed me with her advocacy for women's rights to abortion and her activist work supporting the *Canada Health Act* for universal access to healthcare.

As a friend, she taught me about ballet and opera, played piano for me, yet listened intently to my opinions on family dynamics, love relationships and partying. She tried not to expose her vulnerabilities or anxieties, choosing to watch and admire what she saw as my emotional strengths. We developed that bond between friends who don't see each other often, who end up calling each other at the same time, missing each other, knowing it's time to get together again. She involved me with her sisters and parents and nieces. Though she never married, she always seemed to have intelligent, attractive, unavailable men in her life.

In late 1998, Emma began to fall asleep during her beloved ballet performances. Her friends knew there was something seriously wrong. As was her wont of not 'bothering' another physician, she had blood work done on herself, the results of which were indefinite, so she agreed to see a rheumatologist about her symptoms that included a tender rib cage. His diagnosis was costo-chondritis, or inflammation of the cartilage around the ribs. Then she saw another specialist who confirmed what she herself had suspected by that point: she had multiple myeloma, a bone marrow cancer that in medical school we were taught affected exclusively old men. Emma was 45 years old and female.

With great difficulty, she made it through chemotherapy and two bone marrow transplants. Always playing the clinician, spouting numbers of her blood results and listing medications she was taking with all their possible side effects, she read every medical paper about multiple myeloma.

Her clinical reports on herself and her apparent detachment from the disease astonished me. I suggested she attend visualization classes to help deal with her recovery, as I had done when I had malignant melanoma, but she found them too airy-fairy, too alternative medicine for her. I advised giving up work entirely to channel her energy into travel or fun activities but she preferred to be practising medicine, even if it meant lying down to rest on her examining table between patients.

Emma loved buying presents. During every remission of her illness, she bought more gifts for the fun of spending as much money as she could. She told a friend, "That way, you won't forget me when I'm gone."

For several years, in spite of recurrent relapses, Emma carried on in her professional life. In 2005, she insisted upon travelling to Belleville with an anti-poverty group to sit all day and sign forms for supplemental government funding for food for patients in need. Upon returning to Toronto, she was once again hospitalized.

Her bed was constantly surrounded by her 'Toronto sisters', girlfriends who had known her for decades and supported her alongside her biological sisters. Former lovers appeared at her bedside, after which she would regale us with way-back-when stories of their involvement.

One day when I was sitting with her, she picked up the phone and suddenly her drawn, gaunt face lit up. After a long conversation, she turned to me and exclaimed that the caller, whose name I had never heard before, was the 'love of her life'. Though he lived far away and was married with several children to whom he was totally devoted, they remained in touch. Another ex-lover who came to visit was Elvis Da Silva. He joined the 'sisters' around the bed, joking with all of us, while I was secretly titillated by my special relationship with him.

In the eighth year of her illness, Emma relapsed again and was desperate to be involved in a drug trial that had been cancelled in Canada but funded in Arizona. She flew out to the Mayo Clinic, even managed to get tickets one night to the ballet in Phoenix. Because of a new stress fracture of her hip, she was unable to sit without excruciating pain, so she watched the performance from the back of the theatre, standing on one leg.

One wintery Saturday night, as Janice, Helga and I, three of her 'Toronto sisters', gathered around her hospital bed, she told us she was likely feeling so weak because she 'just had pneumonia and needed to get onto the right antibiotic'—typical Emma, always thinking in terms of clinical medicine. The next day, Sunday February 4, 2007, she died.

One of the first people I notified upon learning of Emma's death was Elvis Da Silva. We talked about how wonderful she was and about our great loss. Later that night, her friends gathered briefly in Toronto but she was buried in Vancouver where the *shiva* took place. Most of her Toronto sisters flew out for the funeral, but my furnace broke down the day she died and I was suffering from terrible back pain, so I couldn't go.

Three weeks later, Janice and I met for dinner at Bar Mercurio on Bloor Street to discuss Emma's memorial and details about the video Helga was filming. I remember exactly what I was eating—delicate venison with yummy corn couscous.

"I'm feeling badly for Elvis," Janice began casually. "It must be hard for him, because he has no one to talk to about Emma."

I reassured her that I had already spoken with him and that he and I were having dinner later that week, when we could commiserate again about Emma and that he'd be fine.

"Well, you knew they were lovers, didn't you?" she asked.

"Well yes, but that was long ago," I answered casually.

"No, right up to the end. In fact, she told me that quite recently, when her bones were so weak and brittle, he'd cracked one of her ribs making love. But I don't think she ever told him."

I was stupefied, but pretended otherwise. My brain was buzzing, my heart thumping. I had no clue he was sleeping with her.

I continued on with dinner as if nothing had happened, focusing on the details of the memorial and the video. I had difficulty swallowing my food, but quickly gulped down a Cinzano and ordered another. Finally, in utter shock, I climbed into my car and drove home.

This was a man I had known and trusted for thirty-something years. He was a friend, a colleague, a confidant, long before he became a lover. I felt hurt, disappointed, betrayed and duped. I realized he must have manipulated both Emma and me for his own gratification. But she had not kept it from her other friends and that's where the breach occurred. It was only with Emma's death that his double secret was disclosed.

She would never know, but I had to go on living with the fallout. I flashed on parties I had hosted, where both he and Emma had attended separately as my friends, where they got to spend time together publicly without questions asked. I was the fool who thought that, out of respect for me, he had come alone, even though I had invited him with his partner. And at times he even blatantly danced with both me and Emma—neither of us knowing about his involvement with the other.

It was all about him. I was mortified. My loss of Emma was compounded.

For several days, I digested the news on my own. My entire world had shifted. Then I told the Toronto sisters one at a time. They were astounded. They told me how Emma had confided about her relationship with El, but he had told her specifically *not to tell Sharon*, ostensibly because he feared it might get back to his partner through me. Her friends knew Emma hadn't told me, so they respected her wishes and never mentioned it to me. Elvis knew both of us well enough to realize that if either learned about the other, neither relationship with him would continue.

Her friends also said that every time Emma was involved with another man, she cut El out, exactly as I had. The sisters told me how they often came to the hospital with food for Emma, and finding Elvis at her side, left, wanting to leave the lovers alone.

Ironically, I knew Emma had a secret lover with whom she spent one weekend a month, suggesting he lived out of town, but she never divulged his name. The sisters told me it was Elvis she flew to meet in Thunder Bay where he consulted as a psychiatrist in an under-serviced area and stayed overnight in a hotel, providing him with a safe alibi for his partner.

It turned out that for 18 years, Elvis insisted Emma and I conceal the same secret. He was having an affair with both of us. He managed to keep us both silent under the pretext that it must not get back to his partner with whom he'd been living for more than 18 years.

In Hebrew, 18 is *Chai* meaning 'life'. So for *Chai,* he had 3 separate lives: me, Emma and his partner. And there were others. I later heard from another of my bright, dark-haired Jewish girlfriends I had introduced him to that he'd also slept with her on and off over the same time period. So that makes four and probably more, given his many sorties to the States, Mexico, South America, Italy and elsewhere.

How could he have so much power over two strong women? How could we be so oppressed, with such a silence between us? How did we let him into our sisterly gatherings and passionate bedside salons? Believing he was trustworthy, we erroneously let him experience first-hand the depth and intimacy of unique female bonding, so he managed to invade and violate the sisterhood.

I reconsidered his live-in partner, Adele. Everything I knew about her was through him, so I saw only what he wanted me to see: an emotional invalid, dependent on him, who would supposedly 'rip him apart financially' if he ever left her. I had no way of knowing whether that was true. She could be just another woman being used by him, providing respectability, keeping him from being available to others and giving him the guise of a stable relationship. The only thing stable about his life was the instability, the ruse, the deception.

I spent hours talking and crying and even laughing about how life is stranger than fiction. I spoke to anyone who would listen. Heterosexual men recalled feeling totally attended to when he interacted with them, as if there was no one else in the universe who could draw away his attention; in return, they 'loved' Elvis. When women met him, they invariably felt he was hitting on them, so they understood his 'deadly charm'.

The men I talked with couldn't understand how he pulled it off. How could he possibly spend all that energy and time keeping his stories straight? And why? they wondered. What was he getting that made it all so valuable? We agreed that we all sometimes tell 'little white lies' to keep things running smoothly, as I had done in concealing my intimate relationship with Elvis. But his was a whole series of convolutions intentionally orchestrated to deceive people he professed to care about deeply.

The sisters shared stories about other men who perpetrated similar types of actions, men who might fulfil criteria in the American Psychiatric Association's Diagnostic and Statistical Manual (DSM-IV) for Narcissistic Personality Disorder, that is—grandiosity, lack of empathy, exploitative with a sense of entitlement, need for worship and excessive admiration. But as Paul Babiak and Robert Hare describe in their book, *Snakes in Suits*, 'the real problem is when narcissistic features shade into antisocial and destructive behaviours. When this happens, the pattern might be described as aggressive or malignant narcissism, which is difficult to distinguish from psychopathy'.

I had loved this man for so many years, had believed he was a real *mensch*. I had so many wonderful experiences with him during the years we were friends and later lovers. I couldn't believe I had been deceived so successfully. He was a physician and a psychiatrist who should know better. I thought about writing him a letter to express my hurt and my pain. I fantasized about shouting it from the rooftops. I decided I had to confront him in person, see his response with my own eyes, because some small part of me still wanted to believe it wasn't true.

Later that week Elvis and I had a dinner date. I rehearsed what I wanted to say. He suggested we meet at Zucca restaurant in the Yonge-Eglinton area, a neighbourhood he preferred where it was less likely that we'd run into people we knew. I suggested he come by my house first. My daughter was no longer living at home so we would be alone and I could speak honestly and openly.

I was nervous.

He arrived, kissed me as usual and started chatting excitedly about Emma's obituary that had just been published in the *Globe and Mail*. A copy was sitting on my side table. We sat down.

"I just found out you and Emma were having an affair," I began calmly.

His face dropped. Silence.

"For a long time," I added. "I'm feeling angry, manipulated and betrayed."

"I guess it was stupid of me. Self-centred," he said, his head down.

"Stupid, self-centred, to say the fucking least! And *both* of us had to keep this secret, supposedly to protect Adele when, in fact, it was only to allow *you* to continue the charade, to have whatever *you* wanted!"

Then he proclaimed that sex was how he was able to feel close to women and that in his family he was used to secrets. He pointed out that I'd agreed to be secretive about our relationship. Yes I had, I admitted, because I loved him and was willing to help protect his partner, not because I was willing to be manipulated so he could also carry on an affair with my girlfriend...

Next he asked how he could help me with my suffering. He knew I would write about it at some point. I replied that I also needed to talk about it... now!

"Not before the Memorial Service," he insisted, his voice getting louder. He said Emma's friends would be at the service and hate him, thinking he was 'an asshole who two-timed Emma'. I assured him the memorial would be about *Emma*, not about him. He shouted at me, saying it might have been all about him in the past, but now I was making it all about me by 'dumping my pain' on him.

At that point, I briskly ushered him out the door.

Shaking, but relieved, I called my girlfriends. They listened intently and assured me he would not be allowed to speak at the memorial as arranged. He would be excluded from Helga's video. And I would definitely be excluding him from my life, as difficult as that loss would be on the heels of losing Emma. Our group's opinion was that he would probably disappear for a while, continuing his Svengali machinations on new unsuspecting women, but would no doubt re-surface years later, pretending nothing had occurred, just as his friend Goldglass had done before him.

Several weeks later, the memorial service was held at the Jane Mallet Theatre, in the St. Lawrence Centre on Front Street East, Toronto. A string quartet played as the hall filled.

The sisters handed out green ribbons in honour of Emma's favourite colour. Friends and family spoke beautifully. Helga's documentary of Emma's life was awe-inspiring and very Emma. Elvis turned up, thoroughly intoxicated. It was hard, but I looked right through him. I couldn't believe he actually had the nerve to show up. I was determined to stay focused on Emma. It was a time for us to mourn, to talk, to cry. But for me, the loss of Emma did not feel real yet...

Until eight months later, when I went out to Vancouver for the unveiling of her gravestone and stood sobbing in the cemetery. Until I stood listening to the singing of the cantor, the words of her sisters, the traditional Jewish memorial prayers of *Kaddish* and *El Maleh Rachamim*. As the 'winds blew and cracked their cheeks, raged and blew', rain pelting us and inverting our umbrellas, Emma was present, so her absence was concretized. And before leaving the cemetery, according to Jewish custom, we each placed a pebble on her grave to mark our visit. As her tombstone reads:

*HER GOODNESS MADE THE WORLD
A BETTER PLACE*

On the plane home to Toronto, I thought about how I tend to describe my life as a whole series of different lives I have lived and how difficult it would be to start my 'next life' with these two enormous gaping holes.

CHAPTER 19

The House that Harry Built...

For the first two years of my life, our family shared a rented duplex on Rusholme Road in downtown Toronto with my father's brother, Jack, his wife and their two sons. My father, Harry and Uncle Jack had arrived from Poland in the 1930s and through hard work and long hours as business partners, built up Dominion Spring, a successful company manufacturing the innards of mattresses. They dreamed of making enough money to build their own homes.

In the late 1940s, they purchased a piece of land together in what was then considered 'out in the boonies', off Bathurst Street midway between St Clair and Eglinton, a large open field with few houses in the surrounding area. They built homes for each family, supervising tradesmen and doing a lot of the work themselves.

On the remaining parcel of land, they planned to construct two more houses to sell, with the possibility of one being a multi-unit dwelling. However, they were unable to obtain building permits for the vacant lot, so were forced to sell. Somehow, the new owner got clearance—illegally, according to Harry—to put up both a duplex and a triplex on the one property. Harry was infuriated by the injustice in his adopted country of which he was so proud, forever despising the absentee money-making landlord whose barren, concrete parking lot and garage abutted our beautiful grassy sloping backyard—a rude reminder of a dispute never forgotten or forgiven.

In March 1949, just before I turned two, the houses were ready so Uncle Jack's family, my parents, my older siblings, Rena and Zel and I moved uptown to Croydon Road. That same day, I met Neil, who was almost three, whose family was moving into a house across the street. Neil and I became life-long friends. Our families also got acquainted and over the next four decades celebrated many life events together.

Many years later, after Neil's father had died and Neil and his older brothers moved out and married, his mother sold their house and moved into a condominium further north at Sheppard and Bathurst. When my father died, my mother refused to leave her beloved four-bedroom home.

Hellie loved the area and prided herself on going everywhere by TTC (public transit). She never learned to drive, not because she feared ferrying five children around, but because, as she often explained, "I don't want to be a chauffeur for *Bubby* Nancy" (her elderly mother who lived to age 103).

Hellie would take the Bathurst bus up to Eglinton, walk to the fruit stores and Nortown Butcher, or bus down to St Clair to stroll the dollar stores and Shoppers Drug Mart. Other than getting some help managing her money from my brother Zel, Hellie remained fiercely independent. Widowed at fifty-nine, she refused to date. She and Neil's mother jokingly shared the adage, "Who wants to wash another stinker's dirty underwear?" Hellie remained steadfastly by herself in her sanctuary on Croydon Road for another twenty-six years.

All of my siblings and most of our children lived in Toronto, so the house continued to be the family focal point. We gathered there for Passover Seders and family birthdays. When any of us returned from a trip, it was there we headed directly from the airport. Hellie would always have a freshly-baked chocolate cake with icing, though she couldn't eat it herself as chocolate gave her headaches. Hellie's house was where we went during the long day of prayers on Yom Kippur, to lie down for a nap on her comfy couches. Hellie's was where we gathered to dress for my younger sister Lynni's wedding and where we took family pictures before my wedding. The photo of a proud Harry, taken at that time, is still the classic image of him that I carry in my mind to this day.

Later Lawrie grew marijuana plants in the centre of the backyard and Hellie—never knowing what they were—took great joy watching him tend a garden so carefully. So many stories from the house that Harry built...

After my failed attempts at being a happy tenant, one of the areas where I considered purchasing a house was close by Hellie's. One Thursday morning in January 2003, Neil, my childhood friend, called to say a For Sale sign had just gone up on a house around the corner from his. It turned out to be a detached 'condo alternative' with two bedrooms, a tiny kitchen and a small back garden at Oakwood and St Clair, exactly half-way between the area I didn't like at Eglinton & Yonge and the one I loved at Bloor & Dufferin.

I saw it the next day. The place was perfect, just the right size. I had no idea where my office would go, but I could worry about that later, as there were several possibilities, all requiring renovation. With the proviso that I not partake in a bidding war, I agreed to put in an offer the following day.

The next evening, while I sat waiting in the car outside the house, my agent went inside to present the offer. Suddenly I noticed a man with a file folder walking quickly up the driveway towards *my* house. My anxiety level rose, wondering if he were the bearer of a competing offer. My agent soon emerged, confirming my suspicions: a better offer than mine had come in, but I still had a chance to increase my bid.

I was angry and stressed to find myself in the situation I had vowed to avoid. The agent tried to convince me to offer my best price one more time and then it would be over, win or lose. By this point I really needed to pee, so I asked to use the washroom in the house. While up there admiring the bathroom, I asked myself what my father would have done. I decided Harry would have said, if you like it, throw another $5,000 at it and then be done.

I went downstairs and did exactly that and the offer was accepted.

The vendors offered champagne. I was thrilled, in a fog, and happily agreed. I wanted to peruse what would soon be my home. The prospect of having my own place, being independent, with nothing but the sky above my head when I slept, was divine. As happy as I'd been to divest myself of home ownership in 1997, my pleasure getting back into it in 2003 was re-doubled. I felt like I'd come home from wandering in the desert for six years.

At age 56, I was pleased to be busy again with mortgages and lawyers and loved being in the driver's seat. Two months after first seeing the Arlington house, I moved in, but the office renovation would take months. I rented a temporary space in a little cottage behind a building on Bloor Street West, where I began work on April first.

Patients were not pleased with my interim office, or its country smell. They were used to a quiet, private waiting room, instead of sharing one with strangers awaiting a variety of therapists, noisy children in tow. But I was happy. In the glorious summer weather, I got to munch my lunch on a private porch, sometimes visited by another GP psychotherapist who worked in an adjacent cabin. It felt like practising psychotherapy in the woods.

In the meantime, work on my house continued. I was building a seventy-square-foot waiting room which had to be supported on six piers of concrete required by the Toronto building inspector. He laid down the law, the contractor laid down the footings and I laid down the cash. After six difficult months of digging and pouring, sawing and hammering, finally, by October, my office was ready. Once again I had to inform patients of a change of venue, but assured them this one would be permanent.

Light streamed into my new workplace through leaded glass diamonds in the front windows and street noises were muffled yet alive. When the weather turned cooler, I didn't have to go out into the chilblain-inducing temperatures to travel to work. I had a lunch hour that seemed to go on forever—giving me time to eat, read a magazine, pick up emails, have a walk, return phone calls and, for the first time in six months, paint my fingernails. The joys of the first day dampened down into routine but the advantages persisted. Having survived the transitional twilight zone, I was reminded of why I loved working at home.

However, my new, peaceful existence on Arlington did not last. I had settled in five minutes from my mother's house at St Clair and Bathurst, just in time to be close by when her health began to deteriorate.

CHAPTER 20

Helpless

Exactly two months after I moved into the new house, mother Hellie, then aged 84, began to feel unwell. A mild discomfort started in her groin, travelled into her back, and every day worsened severely. It was not like her to complain so we knew she must be in terrible pain.

After going out for dinner on Mother's Day, 2003, she couldn't get out of bed the next day. When she stood up, she couldn't bear weight on her left leg and gimping over to the bathroom, held onto the doorjamb for dear life. Somehow she managed to get to her family doctor whose diagnosis was bursitis, for which he put her on bed rest and Vioxx, an anti-inflammatory medication.

I had always been happy to know my mother was in good hands with her general practitioner, a friendly, easy-going fellow whose office was a TTC bus ride away from her home. She enjoyed his bright smile and he liked the *mandel broit* (almond bread) she occasionally baked for him. Those two were good buddies and a working team that I trusted. He booked an urgent appointment with the rheumatologist she'd been seeing for years for her longstanding Sjögren's disease, an autoimmune disorder causing arthritis and dryness all over the body.

I took her to the consultation at an office way up on Bathurst Street. She could barely manoeuvre her walker between the chairs in the tiny waiting room. I had to step over a woman's legs to reach the seat beside her. The receptionist was yammering in Russian to the short, balding, older doctor whose shirttail was hanging out.

When he disappeared into his office, an impatient over-sized woman started badgering the secretary in Hebrew, defending herself for being late again for an appointment. A heated debate ensued, but Hellie, who was usually very astute about what went on around her, remained oblivious. She seemed tense, pre-occupied and not herself. After some time, the doctor emerged, ushering his patient out in Russian and leading us in, in English.

He asked a series of questions and I helped clarify some of Hellie's answers. He did not ask about the walker Hellie was now using to get around. He scribbled a few notes, then, pushing her onto the examining table, checked her briefly. Exhausted, she slumped back down into the chair. Picking up her large brown envelope of X-rays, he flicked a few onto the light box.

"Oy oy oy oy oy," he said, perusing the black and whites. "A lot of degenerative disc disease at L5-S1. And her left hip has a lot of sclerosis, or thickening of the bone. There's Paget's disease, but I don't think that's the cause of her pain. We'll have to get the boys downtown to take a look at these pictures. You're entitled to complain, Mrs Baltman. I'm surprised you're not in more pain. You need to rest in bed, take Tylenol, two every four hours, and continue the Vioxx," he pronounced, rising out of his chair.

I asked about the diagnosis of bursitis that he dismissed as "impossible, because the pain wouldn't be in her groin". I tried to find out what we could expect, whether her mobility would improve. All he said was, "She's not going to be any younger. We'll wait and see after a week in bed."

"What about IV bisphosphonates to strengthen her bone mass?"

"I've seen three people go into shock from that. Don't confuse Paget's with osteoporosis," he chastised.

As he pushed us out the door, I tried one last time: "Well, do we rent the walker or buy it? Do we put a chair-lift in the house?"

"Rent the walker. We'll cross the other bridge when we get to it," he said, patting Hellie's rounded back as she leaned forward on the walker, pushing it out the door. "Try to stand up taller! Stand straight like a soldier!" And as we moved out of his office towards the elevator, he called after us to get the blood work done and call him in a week.

"He said more in there today than I ever heard from him in the past 15 years," Hellie stated weakly.

He had told us nothing new or helpful. We were as much in the dark as we had been when we first walked in. Hellie was practically immobilized by pain and all he could say was: "Oy, oy oy oy oy."

I was disappointed by my own profession for not listening to how seriously affected she was by this pain and how it was not relieved by the analgesics and anti-inflammatories she was already taking. As her daughter and a physician, I could do nothing to help her.

Weeks passed, Hellie continued to be bed-ridden in agony. She developed raw, painful, stasis ulcers on her heels and her bum from lying on her back. She got constipated from the inactivity and from the codeine in the Tylenol 3s she took to help her sleep. Always very active, she found being housebound difficult. Her ankles were swollen. She couldn't eat. She could barely toddle even with the walker.

The CCAC nurse (Community Care Access Centre) said it was due to her arthritis or her Paget's disease. She had contact with her GP by phone, but the prospect of getting into his office was overwhelming. She had all the investigations done to find out why she wasn't recovering: she had a bone scan and more X-rays. There was no response from the specialist's office about the opinion of the 'boys downtown'. She kept getting worse. Still no diagnosis.

My siblings and I were frustrated. We took turns going to see her and found it depressing to watch her change from being a sweet, caring, concerned mother into a self-absorbed, cranky person who could only think about when she took her last pain pill.

We couldn't believe this was the same woman who had lovingly devoted her entire life to her children and family. It was heart-wrenching. And we could do nothing. The medical degree she had encouraged me to get was failing me if I could do nothing to help my own darling mother who had always been there for me.

It seemed that it was all about the diagnosis. Without a diagnosis, there could be no treatment, because no one was willing to pay attention to the severity of her symptoms of pain and immobility. I was angry and disappointed.

I beseeched her GP to do something for my mother who was wasting away in front of us. He said they couldn't have her admitted to hospital for constipation.

This was 2003, during the outbreak of SARS (Severe Acute Respiratory Syndrome) in Toronto, when a new, highly contagious virus, originally from China, was causing a serious form of pneumonia. The frequent news updates were terrifying. Staff at hospitals lined up to be screened for symptoms or signs of fever or cough before entering. In the streets, people wore masks and were advised to avoid hospitals entirely. Doctors and nurses were contracting the disease from patients and often succumbed.

In people over age 65, the death rate was higher than 50 percent. Treatment was elusive. Forty-four people in Toronto died from rapid onset of cough, fever and shortness of breath. Elective procedures in hospital were cancelled, but urgent problems were still being addressed. As much as we didn't want Hellie to be hospitalized, we were desperate to have her treated.

Her health care at home was egregious. The CCAC nurse yelled at her to start walking or she'd never get better. The physiotherapist pushed her to climb up and down the stairs. Finally, some months later, through *schlep* (contacts), my sister Rena got her admitted to the Baycrest Hospital diagnostic unit.

One weekend when my siblings were all out of town, the results were disclosed to Hellie and me. They had discovered a malignancy in her pelvic bone. No wonder she was in pain. No wonder she couldn't walk. The next step was to do an open biopsy to determine the kind of tumour and any possible treatment.

Hellie replied: "I've had a good life. If the tumour is going to kill me, so be it. But I don't want invasive surgery that'll make me sicker, that I'll have to recover from. Especially if there's no treatment once we have a diagnosis. And if there is treatment and it makes me sick, I don't want that either. So I'm prepared to suffer from whatever it is that's in there, and let it take me as it will." Hellie responded with her distinctive elegance and acuity. The staff physician couldn't argue. Her reasoned approach made quality of life the most important factor.

My siblings had to be informed of the bad news upon their return to the city. I told them one at a time: Rena, then Zel, then Lynni, crying our way through it. We had known she was in terrible shape, but we had never faced the brutal fact that she could die. The power of denial was at work in all of us. Once again, Hellie seemed to be the strongest. She had faced her diagnosis realistically and philosophically.

They managed to stabilize her (condition) enough to send her home, referring her to the palliative care team at Mount Sinai, who sent a doctor to assess how best to keep her comfortable without active intervention throughout her demise. After his initial visit, she said: "For the first time, a doctor who listens to me. Finally, someone I can talk to."

Contemplating radiation therapy to ease the pain, she made one more attempt to stay involved with her old GP, calling him to find out what he thought of the idea. He replied that he hadn't received any of the reports, so he didn't know what was going on, therefore couldn't help. He didn't inquire how she was doing, or offer to get the records. She said she felt as if he'd fired her.

Fortunately, the palliative care physicians were marvellous at listening to her issues and alleviating her pain. After several months, we could no longer manage her at home on Croydon Road, so she was admitted to the palliative care unit on 6 West at Baycrest hospital.

Arielle came home from Halifax where she was working on her BA in political science at Dalhousie University and saw Hellie for the first time since she'd been very ill. She was shocked and wept openly, seeing the *Bubby* she'd shared stories with about their adventures on the TTC in such a deteriorated state. She knew she would no longer go to Croydon Road to finish the bowl of leftover chocolate icing from her favourite cake. She, too, had probably been in denial, thinking her mother exaggerated stories of her adored grandmother's decline.

Even with wonderful care, Hellie's downhill course was rocky. Her caregiver, Lucy, was totally understanding, which made our lives easier, but Hellie was slipping away from us and she knew it. We could never spend enough time with her and when we did, she was so different from the mom we had known and loved.

Intellectually understanding the role-reversal doesn't help much. Losing your mom is excruciating, no matter how old you are. The pain is intense. The anger, inescapable.

I wanted her to be there for me. Still be my mom, listening to my every word, advising, consulting, helping. I didn't want to sit with her while she complained or talked gibberish. I didn't want her to leave me. I wanted her back sitting on Croydon Road in her grey velvet chair, watching her TV programs and telling us what she'd learned from them and baking us chocolate cake and chocolate chip cookies and cooking *yushka* (onion-potato soup) and salmon patties. Though I was 58 years old, I still wanted my momma.

The mandate of palliative care at the time was to take on people with no more than six months to live.

Hellie lasted eighteen.

After refusing food for ten days and comfortable on a morphine drip, on the eighth of June, a month she had always dreaded, in the year 2005, with her baby, my sister Lynni, at her side, Hellie took her last breath. After what she'd been through over the previous months, the finality of it was overwhelming. But I believed that it was a sign of Hellie's infinite kindness to others that she gave us two years to get used to the idea of her leaving. It would have been intolerably painful to lose her suddenly.

After Hellie died, the four of us had to deal with the family home on Croydon Road. We had hoped that my sister Lynni might take it over to keep it in the family, but she already had her own home as did Rena, Zel and I. The costs of renovation and upgrades would be huge, so with heavy hearts, we decided to sell.

We had to clear out fifty-six years of detritus from a family with five children. For the next several months, every

Wednesday evening and Sunday afternoon, the four of us arrived at the house, burrowed into the basement and started loading boxes and bags out to the curb, sorted it into recycling and garbage. Other cartons we loaded into our cars to be stored in each of our own basements.

I discovered my notes from medical school in a damp, musty box in the cold-cellar. We uncovered front pages of newspapers from forty years ago announcing world events. We came across a foil package, containing perfectly preserved icing from a cake, which read: 'Happy Bar Mitzvah Zel', who was then 62. We laughed, wondering how the maggots had not discovered it before we did. We found a lock of my brother Lawrie's golden curls from his first haircut, which brought us to tears. We sifted through post cards from Hellie's trips around the world that she bought instead of 'bothering to take pictures'. In every pocket and purse of Hellie's we found her trademark Kleenex and a Mento, sadly reminding us how she always gave them out to the kids. We sorted through collections of formal dresses hanging in basement cupboards, lingerie in drawers, coats in the hall, jewellery in boxes. We each took what we wanted, we gave away stuff, we sold some, we turfed the rest. In record time, we made Hellie's house presentable, even pretty, with its apricot living room and matching Russian blinds in the bay windows.

One week after the house was listed for sale, we descended upon a real estate office on Eglinton Avenue West, hoping to peruse a single offer at 2 pm. What transpired over the next four hours was an echo of the bidding war I had been involved in for my house two years earlier. Two offers materialized and after a couple of exchanges, we took the highest bid, almost twenty thousand dollars over asking price. We were thrilled, until the enormity of the loss of our family home thudded down upon us. The house that Harry built in 1949, that 10 years later he gleefully declared was worth $32,000, had sold almost 50 years later for almost 25 times that amount. Harry would have been proud.

During Hellie's final illness—the first months when we struggled to find the source of her pain—we could get no cooperation or understanding from health care providers.

Once the diagnosis was established and she was channelled into palliative care, her physicians were superb. It left me thinking there are two groups of healers—those who work hard to deny illness, labelling it psychosomatic unless there is a concrete diagnosis; and those who listen carefully to the patient's narrative, accept dis-ease and try to alleviate suffering no matter what.

The experience with Hellie reminded me why I had gone into the work of psychotherapy. I yearned for the time to listen to my patients—to hear their stories and try to help sort through what is going on with them, to help them get relief from their pain. I couldn't fathom continuing to practise with intense time constraints, with limitations from physicians 'on high' who felt they knew better. I had needed autonomy, freedom from being made to feel like the punk every time. Maybe it was facing those arrogant males I'd encountered along the way who felt they knew better than the patient, better than other physicians, especially if the other doctors were women. I wanted to utilize my greatest strength: belief in the power of listening. To be like the physician who had listened to my concern about the benign-looking mole I showed her and by removing it, found the melanoma. "I always listen to the patient," she had said.

I truly believe the patient is always right about their own story. Patients are the experts on themselves. They know better than we do, if only we'd listen.

CHAPTER 21

To Be, Or Not To Be... A Doctor

Out of that competitive U of T medical class of 7T1, I belonged to a group of six who called ourselves 'The Clinic Group'. Over the years, we kept in touch but still couldn't agree on our original connection. Had we shared the same formaldehyde-soaked cadaver in the basement lab of the old anatomy building? Some claimed we were all in the same student group that followed clinicians around the hospital on patient rounds. Others said we were clinical clerks together in final year med school.

Together we'd crept through the sexist halls of the old Toronto General Hospital, the girls with short white lab-coats over even shorter skirts. The boys wore similar skimpy coats wrapped around flowered shirts with long collars, over bell-bottomed, beige linen pants. They sported long sideburns with large geeky glasses. All of our pockets bulged with red rubber reflex hammers, pale green spiral 'Sick Kids' handbooks and deep green vinyl zip-cases containing scopes for inspecting diseased ears, eyes and throats. For testing sensation, we wore red-topped hat pins laced through our lapels. Those were the days when Dr Bruce Tovee led us around his post-op surgical cases, a gaggle of goofs toddling behind the demi-god, catching pearls of wisdom strewn across terrazzo floors:

"Some people go home after they've had their appendix out and think they can just get on a streetcar and hang from the ceiling as it lurches. They pay no mind to the stitches in their bellies being yanked apart. That's why I always tell them, 'After surgery, you're not half as smart as you think you're gonna be.'" One of his many mottos that became well-embossed on our brains.

At some point after graduation The Clinic Group began meeting in a swanky restaurant for dinner every six months.

At first, we took turns picking up the whole tab but I didn't have the resources others did, so when my turn came, I chose a really cheap spot. From then on, we each paid for ourselves.

Later on, the group loved to hear about my dating escapades and in the quietest of dining nooks, gales of giggles would erupt. One of the guys became a specialist, but remained a bachelor, so we teased him about his women. When he did marry much later, his kid was a lot younger than ours, so he was struggling with child care while others were babysitting grandchildren. Another had several clinics around the city. On one of our outings, I mentioned computerizing my billing system.

"Oh, I'd never do that," he said. "With the computer, you're limited in how many names you can put into one time slot. With pencil and paper, I can always add more patients to the list. My staff can even write on the edge of the paper if necessary."

I had moved into psychotherapy by then and explained that it wasn't a problem for me because I only saw one patient per hour.

"Balts, why do you bother to work at all? You only make $100 an hour," he joked. "And how do you stay awake listening to people talk all day?"

Someone else piped up: "Human Growth Hormone, the next treatment for aging."

"I think we actually look pretty good for our age," I replied proudly. And so the banter continued, many years after the original connection began...

In October 2004, a photo of two Clinic Group members appeared in the *Globe and Mail*, still playing hockey after all these years. They'd started in high school, then advanced to the medical school team known as the CJLO or Christian-Jewish Liaison Organization, in which the Jews played friendly hockey against the Christians. Such a divide would never be allowed in the climate of political correctness these days, but it was all good fun and the players became quite accomplished. The *Globe* photo of them, dressed in their old torn hockey socks, with skates too worn to sharpen and helmets yellow and battered, included a caption quoting one of them:

"Not worth spending money on new helmets—you never know when we'll have to quit. As Dr Tovee said: 'You're not half as smart as you think you're gonna be.'"

When the invitation to our 35th medical class reunion arrived in 2006, I was ambivalent about going. I had attended the 25th a decade earlier and witnessed the predictable 50-year-old balding classmates with young, blonde, short-skirted trophy wives on their arms. A few of the med school nerds had turned up with beards and funky glasses, looking pretty cool. Hotties from back then had lost their good looks to lined craggy faces. Some women appeared stouter, dowdier, with dyed hair, others looked as good as ever. But in the end, curiosity won. I couldn't miss the chance to see the baby-faced troupe with whom I had spent six years of schooling, now that they were 60.

As I entered the elegant, usually hushed Park Hyatt hotel in Toronto, I knew immediately where the event was by the loud laughter coming from the lobby bar on the mezzanine level. I joined former classmates and immediately began reminiscing with guys I had sat behind in lectures in Convocation Hall, with people I had sat in front of in the long since torn-down engineering building and with folks whose notes I had copied in the 'new' zoology building, now forty years old and antiquated.

Russell recounted how I had lent him my glasses to see what everyone was laughing about during the lecture by a psychology prof who was always watching the clock. Only with the help of my lenses could he see the Playboy pin-up that some jokers had placed above the time-piece, which was how Russ first discovered his need for glasses.

Bill reminded me of the brutal 9 am Saturday morning 'path chem' (pathological chemistry) lectures, to which we all arrived exhausted from partying the night before and promptly fell asleep until we had to move along to a two-hour biochemistry lab. I had totally repressed all those gory memories.

The voluntary protocol of separation between Christians and Jews, dating back to the silly joke of the hockey competition, was honoured at the reunion, with Jews occupying one side of the lobby bar, Christians the other. As I examined name-tags with graduation photos, some people were recognizable, others heavier or balder or hairier and greyer, while some still retained their baby faces. One guy quipped I'd never talked to him in med school, so why would I start talking to him now? A short blonde woman rushed up and gave me a huge hug. I had no idea who she was until she yammered about Texas and I finally recognized her as the wife of a classmate, Piv, with whom I'd interned.

"Oh my God, you look sooo… American," I blurted out.

"Do you remember the party where you made love with your boyfriend in *our* bathroom?" she shrieked. I didn't know what she was talking about. She went on to relate the story in intricate detail.

For that interns' party, Piv had bought a whole case of Hemingway's favourite Spanish cognac. I knew I hadn't drunk the stuff but was nevertheless determined to remember the name of the brandy.

"Something Doro," I suddenly recollected.

"Fundador!" Piv exclaimed. And we all cheered his memory of partying from thirty-five years earlier.

As we moved into the other room for dinner, I made an effort to break away from my old Clinic Group and sit with people from the other side of the classroom. Their tales proved refreshing. I learned that I'd been known as the youngest person in the class (not true), the girl with the big brain (not true), and the one with the big boobs (true).

I remarked about how different the profession was back then: our graduating class of 186 had only 38 women or 20%; faculty composition reflected a greater extreme—not one female professor taught any of our courses. We talked about how the class had been comprised of mainly white middle class males, very few immigrants or minorities and not a single openly gay person.

Another insight was that because of medical school brainwashing about 'too much competition' between us, we were discouraged from consulting our 185 classmates, who, over the years, could have provided us with valuable referral and collaborative resources.

What I also quietly realized was how serious I must have been about my studies because with all those eligible bachelors around me, I had only slept with one: the man I dallied with in the bathroom and later married.

Buoyed by a rum and coke, I decided to take the opportunity to have a discussion about a more serious issue, one that had troubled me since graduation—to be or not to be... a doctor, and when.

Over the years while on vacation, I had always tried to be discreet about my métier, lest I become the cruise doctor, the Club Med physician, or the island medic. Once, at a spa in Mexico that I visited frequently, a guest with terminal cancer had arrived alone, hoping for a miracle cure. When she wasn't responding to the clear fluids brought to her and was too weak to leave her room, they were preparing to ask me to see her. An acquaintance explained to the spa director that this woman had certainly not expected to find a personal physician at the spa and that I was not there as a working physician, but as a full-paying guest seeking rest. Thankfully, they never called me.

Doctors deserve a break from being non-stop caregivers. It's a depleting job and unreasonable to expect us to perform incessantly from the day we graduate until the day we die. Part of me is tempted to help in order to receive the glory of being 'the doctor in the room', but our Hippocratic Oath states that we must 'Do no harm', so I hang back and feel guilty. We probably don't hear about all the lawsuits involving the heroes who jump into water over their heads. But given the law-and-order tendency in Canada, doctors might someday find themselves getting sued for *not* helping an ailing stranger in a public place. This 'terminal ambivalence' has plagued me for almost fifty years, starting with my indecision about whether or not to apply to medical school, all the way through every moment of my doctoring life. Fortunately my daughter will be free of this dilemma, as she has chosen an entirely different career path.

I turned to Gord, one of the chaps I had rarely spoken to back then, to ask if he'd ever had ambivalent feelings about being a doctor. He stared blankly and obviously didn't understand my question. I tried to illustrate my point by telling him the story of a woman doctor who had just given birth to her own baby. Hearing the cries of another woman down the hall whose obstetrician hadn't arrived, she stepped in and delivered the baby in distress. Great story, since it all turned out well, but what if it hadn't?

Gord replied that he always opted to help because that's what he was trained to do; it was in our Medical Code of Ethics; and he was sure he knew more than the man on the street.

"But what about medico-legal issues?" I attempted.

"I don't worry about that," he said.

Gord clearly did not understand my dilemma and tried to change the subject. Like every other physician in the past with whom I'd tried to examine this troubling concern, he refused to discuss the matter and defended his own behaviour.

My throat suddenly dry, I excused myself, saying I needed another drink. I wandered outside into the cool air, struggling to sort my thoughts about how easily others made the decision to always be the doctor.

Feeling refreshed with a new beverage, I wandered back into the ballroom, where the dance music had started. Then we were called to gather for a class photo to record our antics—still crazy after all these years. To my surprise, I ended up having a fun evening. And finally, later that night, I managed to bed a second member of the class of 7T1, a guy I hadn't known back then. One from the other side of the room!

We all agreed we were looking forward to getting together for our 50th reunion. Though we'll be fewer in number, the University of Toronto will actually cover the cost of our dinners at Hart House. Chances are that by then I still won't be completely uncritical of the profession, ready to overlook our shortcomings or stop questioning. At least I hope not. The long purple fingernails I had to give up to go to medical school are still a part of me, a symbol of the girl I once was and the woman I still am.

Acknowledgements

This book would not exist without the unwavering support of my writing buddy, Laurie Malabar. Her love of the written and spoken word, her critical eye and her brutal honesty kept me focused throughout the ten year gestation. Its birth during the rapidly-changing publishing terrain was deftly managed by Australian author, Julie Harris. Marianne Ackerman, my dedicated editor, prodded me wisely to move from bare bones to full flesh. And long ago, Maureen Jennings mapped out a route for creative expression and paths to deal with rejection and carry on.

For my earliest written words in Israel in 1993, the poet and translator, Rochelle Mass, provided me with mentoring and a manual typewriter; upon my return, Dr Michael Roberts encouraged me to keep writing—thank you both. To all subsequent editors, teachers and consultants my gratitude extends to you—Mark Abley, Bev Akerman, Ann Decter, Jane Finlay-Young, Cheryl Freedman, Lorraine Gane, Shari Graydon, Isabel Huggan, Helen Humphries, Annie Jacobsen, Malcolm Lester, Morty Mint, Liz Pearl, Linda Pressman, Lauren Small and Kent Stetson. Please forgive me if I have forgotten anyone. My appreciation as well to the wider writing community for your positive feedback.

To my entire family—thank you for your support. My mother, gone since 2005, is always with me, and my father still makes me smile. My daughter Arielle inspires me daily and tolerates my passions. My sister Lynni (Jake) has inadvertently honed her own writing skills through all the help she's given me. To my other siblings, Rena, Larry, Zel, Helen, Lawrie and Brian I say *toda raba*. And niece Lila Baltman, thanks for your infectious enthusiasm.

For ten years my friends heard about this project and if they ever doubted its viability they never said. *Merci bien* for your belief in me—John Arnold, Annie Biringer, Maryellen Belfiore, Bonnie Cord, Ena Cord, Karen Dankwerth, Catherine DeVrye, Pamela Divinsky, Christine Dunbar, Ina

Elias, Frank Faulk, Helga Haberfelner, Beatriz Hausner, Marilyn Herbert, Maureen Hynes, Ken Klonsky, Judy Kornfeld, Vera Maidan, Garry Mass, Richard Mongiat, Joanne Naiman, Neil Naiman, Vicki Nakar, Janice Newton, Jim Noble, Avril Orloff, Naomi Raichyk, Susan Reid, Nick Rice, Mark Ripp, David Rothberg, Ruth Simpson, Dory Smith, Charlotte Weisberg, Anne Werth and Jim Williams. A special thank you to Christian Steffan for the excellent cover design and to Jacki Wortsman for the author photograph.

I haven't forgotten my 'Clinic Group' who for years have patiently awaited this book, and whether intentionally or not, have definitely contributed—Drs. Joel Abrams, Howard Bargman, Steve Hanet, Donna Keystone and Lorne Tarshis. Thank you to the rest of my classmates, colleagues and all my patients who have also inspired me.

A warm mention of dear departed friends—Dr Mimi Divinsky, Dr Sasson Nakar, Larry Stanley and Dr Elisabeth Young-Bruehl.

About the Author

Sharon Baltman began writing creatively in 1992 at age 45, using a manual typewriter during a year-long stay on an Israeli kibbutz in an attempt to win a computer in a writing contest. She lost the competition, bought a computer and pursued the long path of studying the craft. This is her first full-length book. She lives in Toronto working as a physician psychotherapist.

24006420R00103

Made in the USA
Charleston, SC
11 November 2013